To Marisol,

Positive *Matters*

Words, Quotations, and Stories to Heal and Inspire

words: helping us reach for success!

Helen Evrard

September 2, 2017

iUniverse, Inc.
Bloomington

POSITIVE MATTERS
WORDS, QUOTATIONS, AND STORIES TO HEAL AND INSPIRE

iUniverse books may be ordered through booksellers or by contacting:

iUniverse
1663 Liberty Drive
Bloomington, IN 47403
www.iuniverse.com
1-800-Authors (1-800-288-4677)

Front cover art by Corby Enfiejian
Back cover photograph by Patrick Connelly

ISBN: 978-1-4759-6361-8 (sc)
ISBN: 978-1-4759-6359-5 (hc)
ISBN: 978-1-4759-6360-1 (e)

Library of Congress Control Number: 2012923562

Printed in the United States of America

iUniverse rev. date: 1/11/2013

To my wonderful twins,
Squeaky and Corby,
and to
Paul, Ahni, Betsy, and Cynthia -
thank you for helping me open the door.

CONTENTS

PREFACE

Once upon a time I was all wrapped up in my profession. I was a practicing medical specialist raising twins by myself in the middle of bucolic Pennsylvania cow country. On the surface, I seemed to have everything. I certainly had a lot more than I did when I was growing up. I lived in an old farmhouse that I had restored room by room, situated on two beautiful acres with a little stream. I was able to start a small garden with vegetables and herbs and had added new shade trees to the lot. I used to sit on the kitchen porch in the evenings and listen to the kids play, have a glass of wine, watch the birds at the feeder, and try to analyze the weather by watching the clouds.

Once upon a time I was making a very good living. My kids went to the local school and, compared to their peers in our rural farming area, were considered rich. I certainly didn't see myself that way. Yes, I had built my own practice, even my own building, but was burdened every day with a sense of noncompletion, and a persistent dread of the upcoming years when the children would be gone and I would be seeing patients day in and day out without achieving some vague, other, greater purpose. I wanted to be able to teach future doctors, to impart my hard-earned knowledge to the next generation. I wanted to be in a more urban environment so I could attend classical music concerts, not have to drive thirty miles to get anywhere, and develop a basis of support to keep me up and running during the latter part of my life.

So I sold my practice for less than it was worth, because

by the turn of the new century no one wanted to buy a solo medical business. I bought a very rundown practice near Buffalo, New York. I knew it was in bad shape, but figured I still had enough time, energy, and smarts to turn it around. How wrong I was.

Immediately after moving to New York State, the thread of my life began to completely unravel. The new practice was in much worse condition than I could have imagined; I had been lied to, deceived, taken advantage of—however you want to phrase it. The commonsense, hard-work approach I took to fixing all the problems simply didn't work. I couldn't seem to find the right help, whether it was my own staff or attorneys, accountants, vendors, consultants, realtors, you name it. I even ended up with subpar medical care for myself and my own family.

Before I knew it, the kids were graduating from high school and I had lost everything—yes, *everything*! I literally bled money—I lost my home, my practice, the furniture, my health insurance, the retirement money I worked so hard to save, my physical health and, eventually, my mental stability. I ended up at the age of fifty-eight in a county mental hospital with severe depression, unable to even pay for my stay. My family didn't want to have anything to do with me. Old so-called friends, who were really just acquaintances, were incapable of helping me out, and in fact were incapable of even comprehending the depth of my loss and despair. I wanted to be dead, but I didn't want to kill myself. I just couldn't see leaving my children with that horrible legacy. I spent a week in the hospital on the locked ward, where I was more or less left to fend for myself. I begged God to take my life, and quickly!

Fortunately, I was able to find a second hospital where the therapists were more interactive. When I was a patient, the focus for depressed patients revolved around de-emphasizing the negative and shifting the focus to the positive. One day, while sitting in the patient lounge, I found a book entitled *The Language of Letting Go*, by Melody Beattie. For some reason it called to me, and I started reading the daily meditations. At the same time, I made up my mind to put the therapists' battle cry of the positive into action by simply making a list of the positive words I read in the book. I wrote them down as I encountered them, whether nouns, verbs, adjectives, etc. Because I considered myself thorough, I decided to write the negative words down too. Before long I discovered several things. Firstly, I found that the very act of simply writing down the positive words *made me feel better*, it made my mood *improve*. In addition, after accumulating a few hundred words in total, I observed that there were *twice as many positive words* as negative in the book. *No wonder I felt better!*

I told my counselors about this remarkable pattern and my belief that working with the words themselves was having a therapeutic effect on me. They encouraged me to continue. After my discharge I searched for a tool to use to easily give myself an infusion, so to speak, of positive words. Being a lifelong avid reader, what I really wanted was a book. I couldn't find one that appealed to me, or that was capable of deeply affecting my emotional state. And so the idea was born that I could create a book to help myself (and others), a true book of "positive words." I wanted it to contain words, of course, as well as the definition and etymology of each. Since this would have resulted in a very short tome indeed, I decided to add uplifting quotations that contain the words. As an added bonus, I thought I would end each entry with a personal anecdote, hoping to inject my thoughts and at times a bit of humor into the picture.

And that is how this book was born. May it be fruitful and multiply. Please pass the positive word along. It really does matter. Thank you.

Helen Evrard
Middletown, CT
October 1, 2012

THE WORDS

ABUNDANCE

*D*EFINITION:

an overflowing fullness; ample sufficiency; great plenty; profusion; copious supply; superfluity; wealth: strictly applicable to quantity only, but sometimes used of number.

*E*TYMOLOGY:

Latin, stem of *abundare*, to abound; from *ab*, from the beginning + *undare*, to flow in waves, from *unda*, a wave.

*Q*UOTATIONS:

Talent is always conscious of its own abundance, and does not object to sharing.

—*Alexander Solzhenitsyn[1]*

Many a man curses the rain that falls upon his head, and knows not that it brings abundance to drive away the hunger.

—*St. Basil[2]*

Whatever we are waiting for—peace of mind, contentment, grace, the inner awareness of simple abundance—it will surely come to us, but only when we are ready to receive it with an open and grateful heart.

—*Sarah Ban Breathnach*[2]

I never thought about this word much. In fact, sometimes I feel it's a bit overused. But it's more in the forefront of my mind now, especially when I think of the abundance of blessings and gifts I've received throughout my life. What came to mind first, though, when I thought about this word, seemed silly: my mother's hair has always been rather thin and sparse, very different from the thick crop I inherited from my father's side. It inspires me to be grateful for the abundance of hair I was born with, so I've got some to spare now that mine, too, has begun to thin as I grow older. My hair is straight—how funny that I always wanted curls or *waves*. I'm simply reminded that when we choose to take a deeper look, we can always find something that is plentiful in our lives.

DELIGHT

*D*EFINITION:

(noun) a high-wrought state of pleasurable feeling; lively pleasure; extreme satisfaction, joy. (verb) to give delight to; to please highly.

*E*TYMOLOGY:

Old French *deliter* and Latin *delictare*, to delight; frequentative of *delicere*, from *de*, fully + *lacere*, to allure.

*Q*UOTATIONS

We do not believe in ourselves until someone reveals that deep inside us something is valuable, worth listening to, worthy of our trust, sacred to our touch. Once we believe in ourselves we can risk curiosity, wonder, spontaneous delight or any experience that reveals the human spirit.

—*E. E. Cummings[1]*

Love is but the discovery of ourselves in others, and the delight in the recognition.

—*Alexander Smith[1]*

Birds sing after a storm; why shouldn't people feel as free to delight in whatever remains to them?

—*Rose Kennedy*[2]

When I was a child, nothing beat the sheer delight of the ice-cream truck coming down the alley behind our backyard in the summer. The neighborhood kids, my sisters, and I would wait at the grass's edge while straining to hear its tinkling little melody, and I never ceased to marvel at the exotic taste of my favorite flavor—teaberry—as I held the dripping cone in my hand. This word brings to mind the innocence and freedom, the sense of letting go and being truly "in the moment," which seems so easy to achieve when you're young. Wouldn't it be nice to be delighted all the time? We need to recall those teaberry-ice-cream moments more often, to recreate those experiences in our mind and evoke those childlike feelings of delight once again.

DREAM

*D*EFINITION:

(verb) to anticipate vaguely as a coming and happy reality; to have a visionary notion or idea; to imagine; to see, or have a vision of, in sleep, or in idle fancy. (noun) a sleeping vision.

*E*TYMOLOGY:

German *traum*, from Teutonic *dreugan*, to deceive. Icelandic *draugr*, a ghost.

*Q*UOTATIONS

Some look at things that are, and ask why? I dream of things that never were, and ask why not?
                                        —*George Bernard Shaw*[1]

Every great dream begins with a dreamer. Always remember, you have within you the strength, the patience and the passion to reach for the stars to change the world.
                                        —*Harriet Tubman*[2]

There are some people who live in a dream world, and there are some who face reality; and then there are those who turn one into the other.

—*Douglas Everett*[3]

I dream every night and usually remember my dreams upon awakening, even if only for a brief moment or two. When I was very depressed though, my dreaming stopped. At that point the thoughts that I consciously generated while I was awake—notions of hope, possibilities, forgiveness, worthiness—assumed a much greater importance than my dreams. Slowly I realized that, with enough effort, conscious dreams *can* become reality. We don't need to search for magical answers while we sleep. Once I made progress on my path of self-improvement, I began to dream again. This didn't solve my problems in a fairy-tale fashion, but it gave me back the sense of being myself. I know that the dreams we generate, whether we're asleep or awake, can provide comfort, familiarity, hope, support, and sometimes—if there's a ghostly encounter—maybe even a good laugh.

POSSIBLE

*D*EFINITION:

capable of existing or occurring, or of being conceived or thought of; able to happen; capable of being done; not contrary to the nature of things.

*E*TYMOLOGY:

Latin *possum* (short for *potissum*) from *potis*, powerful, properly "lord" or "master."

*Q*UOTATIONS

Hold on with a bulldog grip, and chew and choke as much as possible.
—*Abraham Lincoln*[1]

Be kind whenever possible. It is always possible.
—*Dalai Lama*[2]

Nothing is impossible. The word itself says "I'm possible."
—*Audrey Hepburn*[2]

$\mathcal{W}$hen I look back on my life, it seems clear that I put a "not possible" stamp on many things, including my own potential and abilities. Early on in my career I avoided this word when caring for sick people, believing that the hard facts of medicine and science were immutable and a requisite part of a winning game plan. Unproven approaches weren't an option, and good outcomes were simply not possible for certain conditions. As time went by, though, I quickly revised my methods to include the idea of possibility. Finding solutions to a problem became more creative and fruitful. Little did I know that this change was a gift to myself—the very concept that *I'm possible*— allowing me to give more to others in the process.

GENEROSITY

*D*EFINITION:

the quality of being noble; liberality in giving; munificence.

*E*TYMOLOGY:

Latin, *generosus*, of noble birth.

*Q*UOTATIONS

Generosity is not giving me that which I need more than you do, but it is giving me that which you need more than I do.

—*Khalil Gebran*[1]

It takes generosity to discover the whole through others. If you realize you are only a violin, you can open yourself up to the world by playing your role in the concert.

—*Jacques Yves Cousteau*[2]

No one has yet realized the wealth of sympathy, the kindness and generosity hidden in the soul of a child. The effort of every true education should be to unlock that treasure.

—Emma Goldman[1]

∽✼∽

$\mathscr{I}$ engaged in this very positive behavior a lot, often to my great detriment. I can still hear my mother's comment after giving her an expensive gift: "Helen, you're just too generous." How right she was! What precipitated this conduct? Deep down inside I harbored a childlike belief that this generosity would be magically reciprocated— that I would automatically get back as much as I gave. How crazy is that? It was only after I experienced major loss that I recognized the true meaning of generosity; I saw it in the unconditional kindness extended to me by virtual strangers. I still have a generous heart, yes, but have learned to set proper boundaries. Now I can give within my means with a freer attitude, one that's devoid of expectations. Quid pro quo is no longer the paradigm. If someone exhibits that attitude toward me, I've learned to just look the other way.

∽✼∽

EMBRACE

$\mathcal{D}$EFINITION:

(verb) to clasp in the arms with affection; to include as parts of a whole; to take in; to cherish; to accept with cordiality. (noun) intimate or close encircling with the arms; clasp; hug.

$\mathcal{E}$TYMOLOGY:

Old French *embracer*, to embrace, seize; Latin *in* + *brachia*, from the two arms.

$\mathcal{Q}$UOTATIONS

Don't ignore the past, but deal with it, on your own pace. Once you deal with it, you are free of it, and you are free to embrace your life and be a happy, loving person, because if you don't, the past will come back to haunt and keep coming back to haunt you.

—*Boris Kodjoe*[1]

Our task must be to free ourselves by widening our circle

of compassion to embrace all living creatures and the whole of nature and its beauty.

—*Albert Einstein*[2]

We are each of us angels with only one wing; to fly we need only embrace each other.

—*Source unknown*[3]

This word always seemed so touchy-feely to me. "Embrace your plus size!" "Embrace your originality!" I thought that it was subtly urging us to accept something in ourselves that may be different to the point of unappealing, even repellent. But the origin of the word hints at something beyond an individual attribute: when we're embraced, we need someone *else's* arms to enfold us. It suggests the need to look outside ourselves, to move beyond our human bodies and egos. The presence of another is an implied requisite. I always enjoyed grabbing on to new ideas or dreams; I love learning new things. But most of all I like to embrace people. To express the love and emotion we feel for another, nothing beats a big, warm hug.

POTENTIAL

*D*EFINITION:

(noun) anything that may be possible; latent qualities or abilities that may be developed and lead to future success or usefulness; the possibility of something happening or of someone doing something in the future. (adjective) being potent; endowed with energy adequate to a result; influential.

*E*TYMOLOGY:

Latin *potens*, powerful, present participle of *possum*, I am able.

*Q*UOTATIONS

Everyone needs to be valued. Everyone has the potential to give something back.

—*Princess Diana*[1]

Everyone has inside of him a piece of good news. The good news is that you don't know how great you can be! How much you can love! What you can accomplish! And what your potential is!

—Anne Frank[1]

Your past is not your potential. In any hour you can choose to liberate the future.

—Marilyn Ferguson[3]

⌁

This word took on a vast new significance when I became a mother. I remember choosing to raise my twins in a very deliberate fashion, with the conviction that they could "be all that they could be." As I write this, they are both in college, working on degrees that reflect their talent and passion. Mothers possess the instinctive knowledge of a child's capacity to grow and mature, the certainty that her little one will succeed in even the simplest of tasks. I was so absorbed in my twins when they were young, and with fulfilling various other obligations, that I lost track of my own potential. Eventually, catastrophic circumstances took me to a place where I had to look ahead and I had to start the work of healing myself. While seeing the possibilities in others is indeed a noble habit to engage in, we mustn't lose track of ourselves in the process.

⌁

HARMONY

*D*EFINITION:

the just adaptation of parts to each other, or things intended
to form a connected whole; concord or agreement in facts,
opinions, manners, interests; peace and friendship; such
an agreement between the different parts of a design or
composition as to produce unity of effect.

*E*TYMOLOGY:

French *harmonie*; Latin *harmonia*; Greek αρμοσ *(harmos)*, a
joint, joining, proportion.

~~~

*Q*UOTATIONS

Let tears flow of their own accord: their flowing is not
inconsistent with inward peace and harmony.
                                                —*Lucius Annaeus Seneca[1]*

If life isn't about human beings and living in harmony, then I don't know what it's about.

—*Orlando Bloom*[2]

Adversity draws men together and produces beauty and harmony in life's relationships, just as the cold of winter produces ice-flowers on the windowpanes, which vanish in the warmth.

—*Søren Kierkegaard*[3]

I grew up in a musical family. If we weren't singing at church, we sang along with the radio or the record player, we sang on holidays, and we learned to play various instruments. To me, that music was a force that joined the seven of us together a bit more closely than if we'd lived in silence. Now I look for harmony in other places—in the beauty of nature, kids playing in a park, or just a good conversation over dinner. Sometimes we can't wait for it, though; we have to take the initiative and go out and create it.

UNIQUE

*D*EFINITION:

being without a like or equal; unmatched; unparalleled; single in a kind of excellence; sole.

*E*TYMOLOGY:

French *unique;* Latin *unicus,* single; *unus,* one.

*Q*UOTATIONS

We need to continually look within ourselves. Contemplate our inner being and find our own unique voice and then learn to heed it and we will then have the life experience that we deserve.

—*Dirk Benedict[1]*

Cherish forever what makes you unique, 'cuz you're really a yawn if it goes.

—*Bette Midler[1]*

Always remember that you are absolutely unique. Just like everyone else.

—*Margaret Meade*[2]

M

*T*his powerful word allowed me to reach many goals, including that of building a prosperous private practice. My conviction that each and every case was unique—that every problem needed a custom-designed approach—was an essential part of my formula for success in a competitive atmosphere that presented many obstacles to surmount. A tailor-made program was prepared for each person— one that was designed to make them better or give them answers—and I got busier in the process. Although I lost almost all the material things I acquired when I had money, I never lost my ability to see life through the prism of the unique. This outlook helps me remember I can request and receive what *I* need, those singular blessings that will help me along my path. I love the concise pronouncement of Margaret Meade. Yes, I'm unique, just like you!

M

NOURISH

*D*EFINITION:

to feed and cause to grow; to support; to maintain; to encourage; to foster; to cherish; to comfort; to promote the growth of in attainments; to bring up; to instruct.

*E*TYMOLOGY:

Old French *norir*; Latin *nutrire*, to suckle, feed, nourish.

⧸ʍ⧹

*Q*UOTATIONS

Nourish beginnings, let us nourish beginnings. Not all things are blest, but the seeds of all things are blest. The blessing is in the seed.

—*Muriel Rukeyser*[2]

The diversity of the phenomena of nature is so great, and the treasures hidden in the heavens so rich, precisely in order that the human mind shall never be lacking in fresh nourishment.

—*Johannes Kepler*[3]

Pain nourishes courage. You can't be brave if you've only had wonderful things happen to you.

—*Mary Tyler Moore*[3]

What has this word meant to me over the years? Let me count the ways. I spent a lot of time feeding my brain from when I was small on, that's for sure. Twenty-seven years of my life involved school in one form or another. That's an awfully long time! I ate myself silly too, after the twins were born. Besides food, my sources of nourishment became the material things I worked for and procured— my successful practice, a house, a new car, presents and trips for me and the kids. I stopped nourishing the most important part of me—my very soul—and paid a huge price as a consequence. The lesson I learned is to take time every day to water my spiritual garden. I meditate, keep a journal, take a walk, or give someone a compliment or a helping hand if I can. I still struggle with my weight. Some days are harder than others, but I've made a firm commitment to never be so inwardly famished again.

INSPIRE

*D*EFINITION:

to breathe into; to animate; to infuse into the mind; to affect, as with a superior or supernatural influence; to fill with what animates, enlivens, or exalts.

*E*TYMOLOGY:

Old French *enspirer*; Latin *in*, into + *spirare*, to breathe.

*Q*UOTATIONS

Good actions give strength to ourselves and inspire good actions in others.

—*Plato*[2]

A mediocre idea that guarantees enthusiasm will go further than a great idea that inspires no one.

—*Mary Kay Ash*[3]

Keep all special thoughts and memories for lifetimes to come. Share these keepsakes with others to inspire hope and build from the past, which can bridge to the future.

—*Mattie Stepanek*[2]

How could someone who spent her entire life in the world of medicine forget that *inspire* means *to breathe in*? Come to think of it, when someone or something inspires you, don't you tend to take in a deep breath, or maybe even hold it for a second or two? Perhaps the Romans were really onto something. Although this word's origin is the province of the lungs, the modern usage often implies the use of our eyes, either literally or symbolically. We need to look carefully, either within or externally, to find our own source of inspiration. This typically requires some action on our part, although at times help may come unannounced. But when we unearth it we need to breathe out the bad air, breathe in the good, and take the first steps toward healing and fulfillment.

AMAZING

_D_EFINITION:

causing great surprise or wonder; astonishing; very impressive; excellent.

_E_TYMOLOGY:

Anglo-Saxon *amase*, to confound utterly.

_Q_UOTATIONS

May your trails be crooked, winding, lonesome, dangerous, leading to the most amazing view. May your mountains rise into and above the clouds.

—*Edward Abbey*[2]

It's amazing how many enemies you make when you're trying to be a blessing.

—*Kathie Lee Gifford*[2]

It is amazing that the amount of news that happens in the world every day always just exactly fits the newspaper.

—*Jerry Seinfeld*[2]

Initially, this word didn't make the cut to be included in the book. But then I went to a gospel choir concert. At one point in the performance, everyone in the audience joined together in singing this word again and again at the top of our lungs while clapping along to the beat. This was shortly after my hospitalization for depression, and it really elevated my mood! This is a word of a rather vague origin, like *laugh* or *smile*; it seems to have sprung up all on its own. There's so much innate power attached. It feels good just to say it, of course, but don't you usually raise your voice and practically shout it out loud? You smile when you say it, don't you? It may be overused at times, but I quote Shakespeare's *As You Like It*: "Can one desire too much of a good thing?"

RELIEF

*D*EFINITION:

the removal, or partial removal, of any evil, or of anything
oppressive or burdensome, by which some ease is obtained;
succor; alleviation; comfort; ease; redress.

*E*TYMOLOGY:

French *relever*; Latin *releuare*; from *re*, again + *leuare*, to lift,
from *leuis*, light.

*Q*UOTATIONS

And thou wilt give thyself relief, if thou doest every act of
thy life as if it were the last.

—*Marcus Aurelius*[3]

Can I see another's woe, and not be in sorrow, too? Can I
see another's grief, and not seek for kind relief?

—*William Blake*[2]

For fast-acting relief try slowing down.

—*Lily Tomlin*[1]

*H*ow many hours do we spend in life just craving some relief? As a single mother of twins running my own medical business, my energies sapped by chronic depression and pain issues, there were times when I wanted relief from *everything*. I wanted a personal assistant, chauffeur, 24/7 nanny, cook, pet sitter—*anything* to fold the clean laundry, go grocery shopping, schlep the kids around, open the mail—you name it! We all know that life doesn't work that way. Should we just flip the coin? Perhaps if we spend more time helping others, our own appetite for relief would dampen a bit. It's hard to think this way sometimes, but it's always easy to find the less fortunate. Providing relief to others can help us see our own situation in a new light.

EXCITE

*𝒟*EFINITION:

to call to activity in any way; to rouse to feeling; to kindle to passionate emotion; to call forth or increase the vital activity of an organism, or any of its parts.

*ℰ*TYMOLOGY:

Old French *exciter*; Latin *exiere*, to set in motion, call forth; from *ex*, out + *ciere*, to summon.

*𝒬*UOTATIONS

Passion is energy. Feel the power that comes from focusing on what excites you.

—*Oprah Winfrey*[1]

Seize the moment of excited curiosity on any subject to solve your doubts, for if you let it pass, the desire may never return, and you may remain in ignorance.

—*William Wirt*[1]

It is always with excitement that I wake up in the morning wondering what my intuition will toss up to me, like gifts from the sea. I work with it and rely on it. It's my partner.

—*Jonas Salk*[3]

⌢✍⌢

To this day I can still recall the excitement I felt when my science nun, Sister Marcian, taught us about DNA in high school back in the 1960s. She was a fabulous teacher; we used to call her Sister Martian. I credit her with sparking my love of science. I'm so thankful I was able to follow my passion into a long career that served me well and more than satisfied my love for learning. Later on I associated excitement with my children. I can still see their faces on Christmas morning and hear them screaming on roller-coaster rides. I don't need photographs to recall the smiles that erupted after they blew out their birthday candles. Intensely exciting moments may come less frequently as we age, but we can still find sparks in the little things if we just look close enough and call them forth.

⌢✍⌢

SERENE

*D*EFINITION:

bright; clear; unobscured; calm; placid; undisturbed.

*E*TYMOLOGY:

Latin *serenus*, bright, clear, calm (of weather).

*Q*UOTATIONS

For the man sound of body and serene of mind there is no such thing as bad weather, every sky has its beauty, and storms which ship the blood do but make it pulse more vigorously.

—*George Gissing*[1]

Remain calm, serene, always in command of yourself. You will then find out how easy it is to get along.

—*Paramahansa Yoganada*[2]

I feel beautiful when I'm at peace with myself. When I'm serene, when I'm at peace with myself, when I've been considerate of others.

—*Elle Macpherson*[2]

I would never, ever describe myself as a serene person. Behind the façade of a confident, garrulous, and educated extrovert lies a "glass half-empty" personality, albeit one that appears confident and secure. I've always envied serene people; they are blessed with a mysterious inner power. At times it seems to radiate out of them and have a profound, calming effect on anyone else in the room. They attract people like a magnet. This just compels me to plant a serenity seed in my spiritual garden, to water it and nurture it, to see if I can grow some in myself. I believe that you *can* teach an old dog new tricks.

REGENERATE

*D*EFINITION:

to generate or produce anew; to give new life, strength, or vigor to; to cause to be spiritually born anew; to make a radical change for the better in the character or condition of.

*E*TYMOLOGY:

Latin *regeneratus*, from *re*, again + *generare*, create.

*Q*UOTATIONS

Deep, unspeakable suffering may well be called a baptism, a regeneration, the initiation into a new state.
—*Ira Gershwin*[2]

Earth, teach me to forget myself as melted snow forgets its life. Earth, teach me resignation as the leaves which die in the fall. Earth, teach me courage as the tree which stands all alone. Earth, teach me regeneration as the seed which rises in the spring.

—*William Alexander*[2]

Every generation needs regeneration.

—*Charles Haddon Spurgeon*[1]

I'm looking through a microscope again, examining a hydra in high school biology class, fascinated that these quirky little creatures are able to regrow missing parts. I segue in my mind to all the human organs I learned about in med school, and the capacity of each to regenerate. If we didn't rebuild skin or muscle or white blood cells every day, we wouldn't be long for this world! Funny how I never thought I would one day apply this word to my actual *life*, to my very own existence on a day-to-day basis. Well, if it happened to me, it can happen to anyone. I was knocked down, yes, to a place of unimaginable pain, to a black hole of a sort that defies description. But the powers that be allowed me to bounce back again. I've renewed my sense of appreciation for the glorious gift of regeneration.

ASSIST

DEFINITION:

(verb) to give support to in some undertaking or effort, or in time of distress; to help; to aid. (noun) an act of giving help, typically by giving money.

ETYMOLOGY:

French *assister*; Latin *assistere*, to step to, from *ad*, to + *sistere*, to place, to stand.

QUOTATIONS

A man is truly ethical only when he obeys the compulsion to help all life which he is able to assist, and shrinks from injuring anything that lives.

—*Albert Schweitzer*[2]

Make friends with the angels, who though invisible are always with you. Often invoke them, constantly praise them, and make good use of their help and assistance in all your temporal and spiritual affairs.

—*St. Francis de Sales*[3]

To the wrongs that need resistance, To the right that needs assistance, To the future in the distance, Give yourselves.

—*Carrie Chapman Catt*[1]

To assist is to help, there's no question about it. But help can sometimes have a desperate edge. We don't yell, "Assist me!" when we're drowning or when the building's on fire! I spent a lot of time on crutches and in wheelchairs. Someone saying "Do you need help?" often put me on the defensive. I know it was meant in the right spirit, but somehow it offended my sense of independence. "Do you need some assistance?" has a softer, gentler ring to it. No matter which word you choose, we need to fight the anonymous autonomy of twenty-first century living by our conscious efforts to lend others a helping hand. We need to look left and right every day, and "step to" in aiding the needy. You never know when the shoe will be on the other foot.

RESPONSIBLE

$\mathscr{D}$EFINITION:

accountable; amenable; able to respond or answer for one's conduct and obligations; trustworthy, financially or otherwise.

$\mathscr{E}$TYMOLOGY:

Old French *responder*; Latin *respondere*, from *re*, back, in return + *spondere*, to promise.

$\mathscr{Q}$UOTATIONS

The eyes are not responsible when the mind does the seeing.

—*Publilius Syrus*[3]

It is not only for what we do that we are held responsible, but also for what we do not do.

—*Moliere*[2]

If you could kick the person in the pants responsible for most of your trouble, you wouldn't sit for a month.

—*Theodore Roosevelt*[2]

By definition responsibility involves obligations, autonomous choices, and commitments, but we must be careful to keep the urge to control out of the equation. I spent most of my life believing in my capacity to steer circumstances to the outcomes that I thought were best for all concerned. Somehow I equated this with being responsible. Clearly it has more to do with being accountable for your own actions, no matter who is running the show. The beautiful thing about being responsible is that you're acknowledging your accountability to others, yes, but at the same time you're able to keep the promise you made to yourself to act in your own highest good. Publilius Syrus also said, "Never promise more than you can perform."[2] If we live with that in mind, we'd all be able to sleep much better at night.

ADVENTURE

*D*EFINITION:

that which happens without design; chance; the encountering of risks; a bold undertaking, in which hazards are to be encountered, and the issue is staked upon unforeseen events; a remarkable occurrence; a striking event; a stirring incident.

*E*TYMOLOGY:

Old French *aventure*; Latin *adventurus*, fut. par. *advenire*, to come to, happen, to arrive.

*Q*UOTATIONS

An adventure is only an inconvenience rightly considered. An inconvenience is only an adventure wrongly considered.

—*Gilbert K. Chesterton*[2]

We live in a wonderful world that is full of beauty, charm and adventure. There is no end to the adventures that we can have if only we seek them with our eyes open.

—*Jawaharlal Nehru*[2]

I've recently started composting in my apartment, which is quite an adventure.

—*Shalom Harlow*[2]

The many and varied quotations I found for this word were often based on the rather broad themes of life and death. That set me to thinking that we should apply this word to the more mundane things we encounter every day, especially those things that aren't "designed" for our enjoyment, like a late school bus, a traffic jam, or an unexpected snowstorm. These events can make us feel frustrated, angry, overwhelmed, or even afraid. When we're in the habit of seeing such incidents as problems, we cannot recognize them as adventures, as *striking*, *stirring*, or *remarkable* circumstances that may teach us valuable lessons. Perhaps we need a refresher course in patience, tolerance, creativity, or resilience. When not finding a parking space at the grocery store becomes an adventure instead of an annoyance, the burdens of the day seem so much lighter and easier to bear.

THRIVE

DEFINITION:

to prosper in any business; to have increase or success; to increase in bulk or stature; to grow vigorously or luxuriantly, as a plant; to flourish.

ETYMOLOGY:

Icelandic *prifa*, to clutch, grasp, grip, seize.

QUOTATIONS

So long as the human spirit thrives on this planet, music in some living form will accompany and sustain it and give it expressive meaning.

—*Aaron Copland*[1]

If human beings are perceived as potentials rather than problems, as processing strengths instead of weaknesses, as unlimited rather than dull and unresponsive, then they thrive and grow to their capabilities.

—Barbara Bush[2]

Humor is something that thrives between man's aspirations and his limitations. There is more logic in humor than in anything else. Besides, you see, humor is truth.

—Victor Borge[1]

❦

This word has such a palpable sense of action. I associate it with visions of movement and can almost see things erupting from the ground, growing and expanding, turning green, producing flowers and fruit. And yet it was born on a Nordic island of volcanic lava fields, glaciers, and mountains, a rather barren landscape that I wouldn't consider particularly fertile. No surprise, then, that the original meaning is *to grasp*. What do you hold onto to thrive? What beliefs, hopes, dreams, achievements, goals, or people? You might want to write them down for yourself today, be grateful that you have them—and *carpe diem*.

❦

IMAGINE

DEFINITION:

to form in the mind a notion or idea of; to think; to
suppose; to contrive in purpose; to devise.

ETYMOLOGY:

French *imaginer*; Latin *imaginatus*, to picture to one's self,
from *imago*, a likeness.

QUOTATIONS

Imagine all the people living for today ... Imagine all
the people living life in peace ... Imagine all the people
sharing all the world.

—*John Lennon[4]*

The courage to imagine the otherwise is our greatest
resource, adding color and suspense to all our life.

—*Daniel J. Boornstin[2]*

I would imagine that if you could understand Morse code, a tap dancer would drive you crazy.

—*Mitch Hedberg*[2]

Like adventure, this word is often used in quotations. But for me, the first thing it brings to mind is John Lennon's eponymous song, which then evokes memories of his tragic death. I was in my twenties then, living in Philadelphia and driving through a horrific downpour to pick up my relatives who had just arrived from Europe to visit me. I remember sharing my shock and grief with my cousin Claudia from Austria, also a Beatles fan. I was revising this anecdote on the last day of the Olympics in 2012 and was running out of ideas. At that very moment NBC broadcasted the *Imagine* song being played at the closing show, with millions watching worldwide. I believe I'm getting an unequivocal message to let his profound and hopeful lyrics speak for themselves, and for us all.

BECOME

*D*EFINITION:

to pass from one state to another; to be the final or
subsequent condition of; to be suitable to; to be worthy
of, or proper for.

*E*TYMOLOGY:

Anglo-Saxon *becuman*, to arrive, happen; related to
Dutch *bekomen* and German *bekommen*, to get, to befall,
to reach.

*Q*UOTATIONS

We are shaped by our thoughts, we become what we think.
When the mind is pure, joy follows like a shadow that
never leaves.

—Buddha[2]

Wisdom ceases to be wisdom when it becomes too proud
to weep, too grave to laugh, and too selfful to seek other
than itself.

—Kahlil Gibran[1]

All women become like their mothers. That is their tragedy.
No man does. That's his.

—Oscar Wilde[2]

ᴍ

$\mathscr{I}$was raised in the "land of the free," the country where,
in theory, you could become whatever you wanted when you
grew up. The nation where "Be all that you can be" became
one of the most successful advertising and recruiting
slogans for the US Army in the late twentieth century.
I was living proof of this possibility. I raised my children
with this concept firmly in place. So how do you reconcile
this belief with the disappointment that ensues when your
dreams don't come true? Perhaps we can reflect on this
word's origin—becoming what we are could be viewed as a
happening, an occurrence that we may not have envisioned
or planned, but which has put us in a position from which
we learn our own life lessons while teaching something to
others as well. Some gift, some knowledge, *something* of
value is given to us as we follow our path. It's up to us to
simply find it, be grateful for it, and use it wisely.

ᴍ

PROGRESS

*D*EFINITION:

(noun) a moving or going forward; a proceeding onward; an advance. (verb) to move forward in space; to continue onward in course; to go on.

*E*TYMOLOGY:

Latin *progressus*, an advance, from *pro*, forward + *gradi*, to walk, step, go.

∼

*Q*UOTATIONS

Without continual growth and progress, such words as improvement, achievement, and success have no meaning.

—*Benjamin Franklin*[2]

The aim of an argument, or of discussion, should not be victory, but progress.

—*Joseph Joubert*[2]

Progress is impossible without change, and those who cannot change their minds cannot change anything.
—*George Bernard Shaw*[3]

~*~

I regret that I didn't find a way to use this word more creatively when I was taking care of patients. It was easy to draw conclusions about improvement when people took their medicine or made changes at home or work that reduced exposure to allergy triggers. The difficulty lay in helping them understand that when they chose to dismiss the impact of their illness, the disease itself would progress—that their state of health would proceed in the *wrong* direction. We become older as each minute passes; this movement occurs without effort. In other matters we must remember that the coin of progress has two sides. It's when we choose our goals and work hard to achieve them that we have truly *stepped forward*. It can be overwhelming and difficult at times, but it's almost always worth it in the end.

~*~

ENGAGE

*D*EFINITION:

to enlist; to gain over; to win and attach; to encounter; to bring in as associate or aid; to enter into an obligation; to devote attention and effort; to attract and hold; to draw.

*E*TYMOLOGY:

French *engager*, from *en*, in + *gage*, a pledge.

*Q*UOTATIONS

Are you in earnest? Seize this very minute! Boldness has genius, power, and magic in it. Only engage, and then the mind grows heated. Begin, and then the work will be completed.

—*Jean Anouilh*[2]

For in the end freedom is a personal and lonely battle, and one faces down fears of today so that those of tomorrow might be engaged.

—*Alice Walker*[3]

My mother says I didn't open my eyes for eight days after I was born, but when I did, the first thing I saw was an engagement ring. I was hooked.

—*Elizabeth Taylor*[1]

$\sim$

Engage often conjures up the negative for me—I think of people engaging in war or in heated conversations that are not necessarily constructive. I've put a lot of effort into seeing it in a new light, since I had to *actively engage* in the work of recovering from depression. No matter how much others may want to do for you, there's no way around it: dealing with depression or any debilitating illness always reverts back to the work of the individual. In the end, no one but you make it happen. It's not like having a sick appendix or gallbladder that can easily be removed in the operating room while you're asleep. You need to take on the challenge and embark on what may be the most difficult journey of your life. Take that first fearful step by pledging yourself to a future of hope and accomplishment.

$\sim$

FRIEND

*D*EFINITION:

a person with whom one has a bond of mutual affection, typically one exclusive of sexual or family relations; an acquaintance or a stranger one comes across; a person who supports a cause, organization, or country by giving financial or other help; a person who is not an opponent or enemy; an ally.

*E*TYMOLOGY:

Anglo-Saxon *freond*, pres. pt. of *freon*, *freogan*, to love.

*Q*UOTATIONS

Don't walk behind me; I may not lead. Don't walk in front of me; I may not follow. Just walk beside me and be my friend.

—*Albert Camus*[1]

A friend is one who believes in you when you have ceased to believe in yourself.

—*Source unknown*

Outside of a dog, a book is a man's best friend. Inside of a dog it's too dark to read.

—*Groucho Marx*[2]

$\smallsmile\hspace{-0.5em}\mathcal{M}\hspace{-0.5em}\smallfrown$

The experience of abandonment often arises when one enters a state of extreme illness or loss. As my own situation continued its downward spiral, I did reach out to relatives and friends. It was extremely difficult and humiliating, and I was consumed by feelings of shame and failure. In many cases my cries went unanswered. To this very day I am still not sure of the reasons why. At absolute rock bottom I felt completely friendless, which of course was not the case. But then I discovered new sources of help and friendship in many unexpected places. Old friends, too, came to my aid once they discovered the reason for my years of silence. These allies stepped forth to support me in a framework of compassion, acceptance, and understanding, and helped me pick myself up and get going again. To me, they embody the true expression of this word's fascinating origin, since they reached out to me with love.

$\smallsmile\hspace{-0.5em}\mathcal{M}\hspace{-0.5em}\smallfrown$

MELODY

*D*EFINITION:

a sweet or agreeable succession of sounds; the air or tune of a musical piece; a rhythmical succession of single tones, having the unity of what is technically called a musical thought, at once pleasing to the ear and characteristic in expression.

*E*TYMOLOGY:

Old French *melodie*; Latin *melodia*; from Greek μελοσ *(melos)*, music, a song.

ᴍ

*Q*UOTATIONS

Music is the melody whose text is the world.
—*Arthur Schopenhauer*[2]

No vision and you perish; No Ideal, and you're lost; Your heart must ever cherish Some faith at any cost. Some hope, some dream to cling to, Some rainbow in the sky, Some melody to sing to, Some service that is high.
—*Harriet Du Autermont*[3]

I have a "Play the melody" philosophy. It means don't over-arrange, don't make life difficult. Just play the melody—and do it the simplest way possible.

—*Jackie Gleason*[1]

A simple melody, soothing and comforting, can often turn a bad situation into a tolerable one, or at least help you to put it in perspective. It's rare to find anyone who doesn't believe in the therapeutic benefits of music. Why do I find it so difficult to sing along with my favorite CDs when I'm all alone? This seemed to come about as I got older. When my daughter was born twenty-one years ago, she was so incredibly beautiful. She only weighed five pounds when I brought her home from the hospital, but was blessed with huge, soulful brown eyes, gorgeous long lashes, and beautiful skin. Every day I sang Joe Cocker's "You Are So Beautiful" to her while giving her a bath. I should probably take this up again, and sing it to myself. But deep down inside, I'm really waiting for a grandchild.

ENTHUSIASM

*D*EFINITION:

inspiration as if by a divine or superhuman power; a state of impassioned emotion; exaltation of soul; ardent and imaginative zeal or interest; strong excitement or feeling on behalf of a cause or a subject.

*E*TYMOLOGY:

Latin *enthusiasmus*; Greek *enthousiasmos*, inspiration, from εvθεοσ *(entheos)*, εv, within + θεοσ, god.

*Q*UOTATIONS

You can do anything if you have enthusiasm. Enthusiasm is the yeast that makes your hopes rise to the stars. With it, there is accomplishment. Without it, there are only alibis.

—*Henry Ford*[3]

If you have enthusiasm, you have a very dynamic, effective companion to travel with you on the road to Somewhere.

—*Loretta Young[2]*

If you aren't fired with enthusiasm, you will be fired with enthusiasm.

—*Vince Lombardi[1]*

Enthusiasm disappears from your vocabulary quite quickly when depression takes over. At my lowest point I, like many others with this illness, had to force myself to brush my teeth, and getting up off the couch wasn't even an option. But as I started to get better, little sparks of interest began to pop up here and there—the twinkling light in my dog's eyes, a beautiful sunset, the cheerful songs of birds in early morning. When things are bleak we need to find these sparks and blow on them gently, turning the kindling of our hopes and dreams into the warm, glowing fire of a real outcome. Gradually (or perhaps suddenly) we'll discover our passion and excitement again, and then we'll have been truly blessed by God.

SUSTAIN

Definition:

to keep from falling; to support; to uphold; to maintain;
to aid, comfort, or relieve; to endure without failing or
yielding; to bear up under; to keep from sinking, as in
despondence, or the like.

Etymology:

French *soutenir*; Latin *sustinere*, from *sus*, extension of *sub*,
up + *tenere*, to hold.

Quotations

To live only for some future goal is shallow. It's the sides
of the mountain that sustain life, not the top.

—*Robert M. Pirsig*[2]

Man's ultimate destiny is to become one with the Divine
Power which governs and sustains the creation and its
creatures.

—*Alfred A. Montapert*[3]

The clear-sighted do not rule the world, but they sustain and console it.

—*Agnes Repplier*[1]

CRYC

This word is so heavy with intense significance for me that it's hard to even reflect on it. It brings up painful memories of my time in the psych ward when my depression was at its very worst, at which point I had to dig deep inside and ask myself what was sustaining me, what was keeping me alive. I wanted to be dead, absolutely, but not by my own hand. I know that the unconditional love of my son was the force that held my head above water—the love of an eighteen-year-old young man who watched his mother lose everything but who never judged me, never blamed me, who always stood by my side. As I slowly got better, I realized he provided me with an invaluable life lesson in forgiveness, compassion, and forbearance. Child teaching mother? You bet! A miraculous event for which I am eternally grateful.

CRYC

CHERISH

*D*EFINITION:

to treat with tenderness and affection; to nurture with care; to hold dear; to embrace with interest; to indulge; to encourage; to foster; to promote.

*E*TYMOLOGY:

Old French *cherir*, to hold dear; Latin *carus*, dear.

*Q*UOTATIONS

I value the friend who for me finds time on his calendar, but I cherish the friend who for me does not consult his calendar.

—*Robert Braut*[3]

Make the most of your regrets; never smother your sorrow, but tend and cherish it till it comes to have a separate and integral interest. To regret deeply is to live afresh.

—*Henry David Thoreau*[3]

Take your victories, whatever they may be, cherish them, use them, but don't settle for them.

—*Mia Hamm*[1]

$\mathscr{M}$ost of the "cherish" quotations I found were conceptual in nature, and spoke of dreams, hopes, ideals, and other such notions. But I usually associate this word with objects and things, with the keepsakes, mementos, and other tangible items that we hold dear. What do you cherish more, your thoughts and ideas, or the little knickknacks on your shelf? A time came for me when I had to scale back to the bare minimum. I lost so many objects that harbored memories of times gone by. But they were only things. Now I search for new tchotchkes that represent beliefs, intentions, goals, or ideals. Either way, I've learned that *cherish* can apply to tomorrow as much as it does to yesterday.

ADVANCE

$\mathcal{D}$EFINITION:

(verb) to move forward; to make to go on; to help on; to bring to view or notice. (noun) improvement or progression, physically, mentally, morally, or socially; the first step toward the attainment of a result.

$\mathcal{E}$TYMOLOGY:

Old French *avancer*, to go before; from Latin *ab*, from + *ante*, before.

$\mathcal{Q}$UOTATIONS

There is no finer sensation in life than that which comes with victory over one's self. Go forward to a goal of inward achievement, brushing aside all your old internal enemies as you advance.

—*Vash Young*[3]

There is no road too long to the man who advances deliberately and without undue haste; there are no honors too distant to the man who prepares himself for them with patience.

—*Jean de la Bruyere*[1]

If I planned out everything in advance, I'd expire of boredom.

—*Peter Straub*[1]

⌒⁂⌒

I lived in a world of "advances" when I was practicing medicine. Part of my job was to keep up with the latest treatment for allergies, the most recent test or scan, the newest breakthrough in asthma. Over time I learned that I could help people just as well by using older, tried and true methods, that those current recommendations by the expert du jour were not necessarily better. I certainly had to revisit this word when life as I knew it came to a grinding halt. I was dead in the water; the word became a verb instead of a noun. At that point, *I* had to advance, all by myself, in a deliberate and painstakingly slow fashion. But each of us possesses this capability. We can indeed take the first step toward a better day. The future is waiting before us.

⌒⁂⌒

PROCEED

*D*EFINITION:

to move, pass, or go forward or onward; to advance; to pass from one point, topic, or stage to another; to come from; to begin and carry on a series of acts or measures.

*E*TYMOLOGY:

Old French *proceder*; Latin *procedere*, from *pro*, before + *cedere*, to go.

*Q*UOTATIONS

Our duty, as men and women, is to proceed as if limits to our ability did not exist. We are collaborators in creation.
—*Pierre Teilhard de Chardin*[2]

Begin to free yourself at once by doing all that is possible with the means you have, and as you proceed in this spirit the way will open for you to do more.
—*Georges Clemenceau*[2]

The difficulties you meet will resolve themselves as you advance. Proceed, and light will dawn, and shine with the increasing clearness on your path.

—Jean-Baptiste D'Alembert[3]

*H*ere's another word about moving forward. You will find it in the thesaurus as a synonym for progress. So why do I include them both in this book? Well, why not? Reminding ourselves of a positive idea, repeating a good thing—we use these tools as affirmations, of course. There is no option to stay stagnant. As humans we *will* proceed, we *must* move forward, we travel further along the path of life with every breath we take. Choice enters the picture in the *way* that we do this. We can create obstacles and make things difficult for ourselves and others, or we can operate from a posture of compassion, forgiveness, and self-love. Deliberate and conscious decisions can help to smooth the way, not matter how many times we fall.

PROVIDE

*𝒟*EFINITION:

to look out for in advance; to prepare; to supply; to contribute; to take measures beforehand in view of an expected or possible future need.

*ℰ*TYMOLOGY:

Latin *providere*, to foresee, from *pro*, before + *videre*, to see.

*𝒬*UOTATIONS

He that planteth a tree is a servant of God, he provideth a kindness for many generations, and faces that he hath not seen shall bless him.

—*Henry Van Dyke[1]*

Old people like to give good advice, as solace for no longer being able to provide bad examples.

—*François de la Rochefoucauld[1]*

Sound character provides the power with which a person may ride the emergencies of life instead of being overwhelmed by them. Failure is ... the highway to success.

—*Augustine (Og) Mandino*[3]

A mousetrap always provides free cheese.

—*Source unknown*[3]

჻

My success was self-made all along the way. I borrowed and worked my way through college and med school, and I was in solo practice for my entire career. I always provided for myself. What, then, did I have to fall back on when everything I worked for was gone? How many times in my downward spiral did the question "Who will provide for *me*?" re-echo in my mind? Entirely too many times, I'm afraid. Late into my fifties I had to face a horrific and inevitable "Now what?" I sought and received help from the government, since other avenues were closed to me. Now I'm taking steps to be self-sufficient again, to prepare myself for "possible future needs." If others can do it, I can too. To quote George Eliot: "It is never too late to be what you might have been."[1]

჻

FEAST

*D*EFINITION:

(noun) a festival; a holiday; a festive or joyous meal; a grand, ceremonious, or sumptuous entertainment; that which is partaken of, or shared in, with delight. (verb) to eat sumptuously; to be highly gratified or delighted.

*E*TYMOLOGY:

Old French *feste*; Latin *festum*, a feast, orig. neuter of *festus*, joyful.

*Q*UOTATIONS

All our words are but crumbs that fall down from the feast of the mind.

—*Kahlil Gibran*[1]

Don't get up from the feast of life without paying for your share of it.

—*Dean William Inge*[2]

Thanksgiving is America's chow-down feast, the one occasion each year when gluttony becomes a patriotic duty.

—*Michael Dresser*[1]

I could never have imagined that this word derives from "joy," but then again, don't we all feel happy after a good meal or a catered event? Ironically, after my twins were born I "celebrated" for years by eating myself into a state of clinical obesity. Of course I was really eating for other reasons, and to this very day I'm still trying to work that out. In putting effort into undoing that dreadful behavior, I'm reminding myself that I can feast in many other ways. I can enjoy nature's beauty while taking a walk. I can spend time with my children or friends, or just relax on the couch and read a good book. And I've learned that sharing a few kind words with others can be a feast for a hungry soul.

AGREE

_D_EFINITION:

to harmonize in opinion, statement, or action; to be in unison or concord; to concur; to come to terms or to a common resolve; to make harmonious; to reconcile or make friends.

_E_TYMOLOGY:

Old French, _agréer_, from _a gré_, according to one's pleasure; from Latin _ad_, to + _gratus_, pleasing.

_Q_UOTATIONS

No two on earth in all things can agree. All have some daring singularity.

—_Sir Winston Churchill_[3]

Agreeing to disagree is a way of giving up—an admission that neither one of us has the skills, courage, or tenacity to work it out!

—_Suzanne Mayo Frindt_[3]

It's no good agreeing with a person who can't make up his mind.

—*Source unknown*[3]

Too much agreement kills a chat.

—*Eldridge Cleaver*[3]

⌘

I know people who seem to enjoy conflict, but I myself avoid fights like the plague. I grew up in a home where my parents simply did not wage that many battles. I'm not passive, by any means, and at times it can appear that I simply must have it my way. Be that as it may, my approach in dealing with others has always been to arrive at a place of agreement. I consciously choose to acknowledge differences of opinion, and to approach people and issues in a nonjudgmental fashion. Agreeing first and foremost to work toward some common ground, to come to a consensus, can be a most pleasing and rewarding endeavor. If we combine this approach with some compromise and sacrifice, it'll all work out in the end.

⌘

TOLERANCE

*𝒟*EFINITION:

the power or capacity of enduring; the endurance of the presence or actions of objectionable persons, or of the expression of offensive opinions.

*ℰ*TYMOLOGY:

Middle French *tolerance*; Latin *tolerantia*, from *tolerare*, to endure; allied to *tollere*, to lift, bear.

*𝒬*UOTATIONS

In the practice of tolerance, one's enemy is the best teacher.

—*The Dalai Lama*[3]

The test of courage comes when we are in the minority. The test of tolerance comes when we are in the majority.

—*Ralph W. Sockman*[3]

When traveling with someone, take large doses of patience and tolerance with your morning coffee.

—*Helen Hayes*[1]

This word is so very dear to my heart because I have a gay son. Long before the phenomenon of bullying achieved national prominence, I wrung my hands in anguish as he endured various forms of physical and verbal abuse in middle school. This was among the reasons I left Pennsylvania and started a new endeavor in Buffalo, not knowing that this decision would have very dire consequences for us all. But I'd do it all again in a heartbeat. Fortunately, I was able to provide him and his sister with a first-rate and safe high school experience. As my world collapsed, I was also able to discover my own inner strength and resilience. All three of us weathered the storm, we endured, and as far as I can tell, we're all the better because of it.

SECURE

*D*EFINITION:

(adjective) free from fear, care, or anxiety; not feeling suspicion or distrust; not exposed to danger; safe. (verb) to make safe; to relieve from apprehensions of, or exposure to, danger; to put beyond hazard of losing or of not receiving.

*E*TYMOLOGY:

Latin *securus*, from *se*, free from + *cura*, anxiety.

*Q*UOTATIONS

Life is made up, not of great sacrifices or duties, but of little things, in which smiles and kindness, and small obligations given habitually, are what preserve the heart and secure comfort.

—Sir Humphry Davy[3]

Consider the postage stamp, my son. It secures success through its ability to stick to one thing till it gets there.

—Josh Billings[3]

The fly that doesn't want to be swatted is most secure when it lights on the fly swatter.

—*Georg C. Lichtenberg*[2]

⚜

*S*o many words that I've chosen for this book seem to have a "before" and "after" meaning to me. This is one of them. I had built what I thought was a secure situation before I lost it all. I built it the old-fashioned way, with education, hard work, savings—the usual stuff. At the top of my game I had a home, a retirement plan, health insurance, credit cards—more than enough to feel safe from harm. It seemed to evaporate so quickly, despite a herculean effort on my part to hold on. The "after" significance is that I am now more secure in *myself*—the work I've put in to heal my soul has truly put me beyond the hazard of not receiving. I count my blessings often, and I am grateful for them every day. When times are tough, I remind myself of the humble little postage stamp.

⚜

CONNECT

$\mathscr{D}$EFINITION:

to join, or fasten together; to unite or link; to cohere; to establish a bond or relation between; to associate (a person or thing, or one's self) with another person, thing, business, or affair.

$\mathscr{E}$TYMOLOGY:

Latin *connectere*; from *con*, together + *nectere*, to bind, tie, knit, join.

$\sim\!\!\mathscr{M}\!\!\sim$

$\mathscr{Q}$UOTATIONS

A great attitude does much more than turn on the lights in our worlds; it seems to magically connect us to all sorts of serendipitous opportunities that were somehow absent before the change.

—*Earl Nightingale*[3]

The most basic and powerful way to connect to another person is to listen. Just listen. Perhaps the most important thing we ever give each other is our attention. ... A loving silence often has far more power to heal and to connect than the most well-intentioned words.

—Rachel Naomi Remen[3]

As we get past our superficial material wants and instant gratification we connect to a deeper part of ourselves, as well as to others, and the universe.

—Judith Wright[2]

Have you ever stopped to wonder about your strongest connections? A list of relationships springs instantly to the forefront. I've had many over the years—some stronger than others, some long, some short, of myriad shapes and sizes. I have an unbreakable connection to my children, of course, and had the predictable business and professional attachments. But the ironclad, unassailable connection to my rational mind was the one I had to soften, so that I could fashion and nurture a new bond with my spiritual and physical self. My state of imbalance had almost destroyed me, but by forging new ties with those muted resources, I discovered the strength to move on.

GRATEFUL

*D*EFINITION:

having a due sense of benefits received; willing to acknowledge and repay, or give thanks for, benefits.

*E*TYMOLOGY:

Latin *gratus*, pleasing + Anglo-Saxon *–ful*, full.

*Q*UOTATIONS

A simple grateful thought turned heavenwards is the most perfect prayer.

—*Doris Lessing*[3]

Animals are reliable, many full of love, true in their affections, predictable in their actions, grateful and loyal. Difficult standards for people to live up to.

—*Alfred A. Montepert*[2]

When we were children we were grateful to those who filled our stockings at Christmas time. Why are we not grateful to God for filling our stockings with legs?

—*Gilbert K. Chesterton[1]*

All world religions endorse the habit of gratitude for anyone following a spiritual path. Sadly, its importance was lost on me for many years. I spent decades caring for sick people, a complicated and time-consuming task that caused fatigue and frustration, with my good intentions being frequently impeded by the bureaucracy of the health-care system. I remember many days when I wondered why no one had personally thanked me for my help. I often felt taken for granted. Now it's not about me expecting thanks from others, it's about the conscious awareness of the blessings I'm graced with every day. Indeed, I sit in profound gratitude that I'm still on this earth to enjoy them!

CONSIDER

DEFINITION:

to fix the mind on, with a view to a careful examination; to ponder; to look at attentively; to pay due attention to; to think seriously; to reflect; to deliberate.

ETYMOLOGY:

Old French *considerer*; Latin *considerare*, to observe, orig. to inspect the stars, from *con*, together + *sidus*, a star, a constellation.

QUOTATIONS

What the mind attends to, the mind considers. What the mind constantly considers, the mind believes. What the mind believes, the mind eventually does.

—Source unknown[3]

Consider how much more you often suffer from your anger and grief, than from those very things for which you are angry and grieved.

—Marcus Antonius[3]

Old age isn't so bad when you consider the alternative.
—*Maurice Chevalier*[2]

I don't consider myself bald, I'm just taller than my hair.
—*Lucius Annaeus Seneca*[2]

In the world of medicine I quickly learned that it is virtually impossible to take everything into consideration when you're helping sick people. There are just too many elements and too little time. Years of knowledge, training, and experience allowed me to make many, many decisions every day, often automatically. Thought processes become almost like an unconscious reflex at times, but that's the nature of the beast. When that part of my life evaporated I received an unexpected gift—*more* than enough time to examine my thoughts, behaviors, beliefs, and dreams. I now have time to truly consider ... practically *everything*! As I continue my work toward balance and health, I must remember to always give myself time to think of, and reach for, the stars.

DISCERN

*D*EFINITION:

to see or understand the difference; to make distinction; to see by the eye or by the understanding; to perceive and recognize.

*E*TYMOLOGY:

Old French *discerner*; Latin *discernere*, to distinguish, from *dis*, apart + *cernere*, to separate.

*Q*UOTATIONS

As far as we can discern, the sole purpose of human existence is to kindle a light in the darkness of mere being.

—*Carl Jung*[3]

All things entail rising and falling timing. You must be able to discern this.

—*Miyamoto Musashi*[2]

The eye by long use comes to see even in the darkest cavern: and there is no subject so obscure but we may discern some glimpse of truth by long poring on it.

—George Berkeley[2]

Did you ever envy someone's discerning judgment, their seemingly effortless ability to see things in a deep and penetrating way? At times, I've been amazed by people who can distinguish a fine wine from the average offering, a piece of good furniture from a solid reproduction. But look at this word's origin—it actually means *to separate*. When I think I've discerned a deep meaning or lesson, I pretty much take it as a whole. I don't split it up into separate components, each of which may have a valuable lesson that I would otherwise miss. Think about this the next time you feel you've been uncommonly perceptive. You may just be missing something.

INNOVATE

*D*EFINITION:

to bring in as new; to change or alter by introducing something new; to remodel; to revolutionize.

*E*TYMOLOGY:

Latin *innovare*, from *in*, in + *novare*, to make new.

*Q*UOTATIONS

Sometimes when you innovate, you make mistakes. It is best to admit them quickly, and get on with improving your other innovations.

—Steve Jobs[1]

You have all the reason in your world to achieve your grandest dreams. Imagination plus innovation equals realization.

—Denis Waitley[3]

Without change there is no innovation, creativity, or incentive for improvement. Those who initiate change

will have a better opportunity to manage the change that
is inevitable.

—*William Pollard*[2]

When you innovate, you've got to be prepared for everyone
telling you you're nuts.

—*Larry Ellison*[2]

꧁꧂

Oh, the miracle of modern advertising, that massive
machine that conditions us to constantly crave the products
of innovation. We just *have to have* the latest phone,
fragrance, designer clothes, computer accessories, whatever.
We simply cannot miss that reality show season premier;
we can't download music from the latest breakthrough
artist fast enough. The benefits and shortcomings of the
technological revolution almost go without saying, and
we rely on its practical output to get us through the day.
But we don't often apply the practice of innovation to our
spiritual lives. We're unaware of the transformation that
can occur if we do. All I know now is that the "me" that
emerged from the ashes of loss and depression is indeed
quite new and improved.

꧁꧂

REVELATION

*D*EFINITION:

the act or revealing, disclosing, or discovering to others what was previously unknown to them; the act of revealing divine truth.

*E*TYMOLOGY:

Middle French, *reveler*; Latin *revelare*, to unveil, draw back a veil, from *re*, back + *velare*, to veil.

*Q*UOTATIONS

Experience is a revelation in the light of which we renounce our errors of youth for those of age.

—*Ambrose Bierce*[3]

Nature is the true revelation of the Deity to man. The nearest green field is the inspired page from which you may read all that it is needful for you to know.

—*Sir Arthur Conan Doyle*[1]

Minor things can become moments of great revelation when encountered for the first time.

—*Margot Fonteyn*[2]

There can be no keener revelation of a society's soul than the way in which it treats its children.

—*Nelson Mandela*[2]

This word makes me think of an *aha* moment, a sudden bolt of lightning that erupts from roiling clouds as a deep male voice makes a grave pronouncement. What I've learned, though, is to pay attention to subtle guidance, secrets, or insights that can be revealed at a moment's notice. I think Conan Doyle is right: nature can be a marvelous source of this wisdom. Just think of how much we can learn from a dandelion, a sparrow, or an ant, if we consciously choose to pay attention? I developed a new appreciation of air when I read that it is the first gift we receive when we're born, even before a mother's touch, and is the last one we are given before we leave this earthly realm. I've never thought of air the same since! When things don't go my way or I'm just having a bad day, I try to pull back my own veil of impatience and ignorance to search for the lessons and blessings that are there to unearth.

COMPANION

$\mathscr{D}$EFINITION:

one who accompanies another for a longer or shorter period, either from choice or casually; one who is much in the company of, or is associated with, another or others; an associate; a comrade; a partner.

$\mathscr{E}$TYMOLOGY:

Old French *companion*; Late Latin *companiem*, a taking of meals together, from *cum*, with + *panis*, bread.

$\mathscr{Q}$UOTATIONS

Hope is the companion of power, and mother of success; for who so hopes strongly has within him the gift of miracles.

—*Samuel Smiles*[3]

If you have enthusiasm, you have a very dynamic, effective companion to travel with you on the road to Somewhere.

—*Loretta Young*[1]

Our perfect companions never have fewer than four feet.
—*Sidonie-Gabrielle Colette*[1]

⌒✺⌒

*L*ess than two months after my twins left for college, I lost my home. I hadn't worked for over six months, and couldn't make the mortgage payment. In a very abrupt fashion I found myself with no one by my side except my faithful companion, Tippy, my baby girl, an adorable black and white Lhasapoo. When my daughter was ten years old she dragged me to the pet store to look at albino frogs. Since I knew what would happen if I brought them into a home with two cats, I refused to take the bait. But in the back of the store we found Tippy, shivering miserably in her crate, the only puppy left in the store that day. She was an impulse buy, yes, but we couldn't turn our backs. She brightened every day, and did indeed share my meals and snacks when I ended up isolated and alone. I'm thankful that she was able to see me through the worst, my faithful partner until her unforeseen passing after ten years of loving service.

⌒✺⌒

SPLENDID

DEFINITION:

shining; very bright; showy; magnificent; sumptuous; heroic; celebrated; brilliant.

ETYMOLOGY:

French *splendide*; Latin *splendidus*, shining, bright.

QUOTATIONS

Nothing splendid has ever been achieved except by those who dared believe that something inside them was superior to circumstance.

—Bruce Barton[2]

Life has loveliness to sell, all beautiful and splendid things, blue waves whitened on a cliff, soaring fire that sways and sings, and children's faces looking up, holding wonder like a cup.

—Sara Teasdale[1]

I have long been of the opinion that if work were such a splendid thing the rich would have kept more of it for themselves.

—*Bruce Grocott*[2]

⁓

This word didn't make the initial cut, but then my brother suggested I include it and I changed my mind. The first thing that comes to mind about splendid is how very rarely we use it! What a beautiful, positive word; I can't see anything bad about it. I think the British more commonly use it. If I recall correctly, my friend Paul, a gifted shaman and counselor, used it quite a bit when I did some work with him before I started this book. He also said "gobsmacked" a lot when he spoke about being surprised or taken aback. Ouch! That word even *sounds* painful! But *splendid*, with its lovely root in shining lights and brilliance, is undeniably a word we should try to use more often.

⁓

TRUST

DEFINITION:

(noun) assured resting of the mind on the integrity, veracity, justice, friendship, or other sound principle, of another person; hope; belief. (verb) to place confidence in; to rely on, to confide or repose faith in.

ETYMOLOGY:

Icelandic *traust*, trust, protection, firmness; German *trost*, comfort, consolation, help, protection.

QUOTATIONS

As for courage and will—we cannot measure how much of each lies within us, we can only trust there will be sufficient to carry through trials which may lie ahead.

—*Andre Norton*[3]

All I have seen teaches me to trust the creator for all I have not seen.

—*Ralph Waldo Emerson*[2]

It is better to suffer wrong than to do it, and happier to be sometimes cheated than not to trust.

—*Samuel Johnson*[1]

Never trust a computer you can't throw out a window.
—*Steve Wozniak*[3]

In the first draft of this book, I actually wrote an entry for this word twice. While working on it the second time, I had a feeling of déjà vu. The quotations had a vague sense of familiarity. Imagine my shock when I realized I'd done it before—even the anecdote was eerily similar! At that time I was making plans to move from Buffalo to Connecticut and almost didn't make my third trip down to scout out housing. I believed no one would approve my apartment application, since I'd failed on prior trips because of my poor credit history. Now I feel I was *meant* to revisit this word at exactly a point in time when I needed it most, when I needed to *trust* that a higher power would smooth the way for me. An apartment materialized on that final trip! In the past, the trust I had naively placed in others had caused terrible losses and prompted me to become suspicious and fearful. My hand was guided to scrutinize this word twice, which has helped me to put faith in others again.

APPRECIATE

$\mathcal{D}$EFINITION:

to set a price or value on; to estimate justly; to value; to be sensible of; to distinguish.

$\mathcal{E}$TYMOLOGY:

Latin *appretiare*, from *ad*, to + *pretium*, price.

$\mathcal{Q}$UOTATIONS

Let us learn to appreciate there will be times when the trees will be bare, and look forward to the time when we may pick the fruit.

—*Anton Chekov[1]*

I do believe that if you haven't learnt about sadness, you cannot appreciate happiness.

—*Nana Mouskouri[2]*

Knowing trees, I understand the meaning of patience. Knowing grass, I can appreciate persistence.

—*Hal Borland[2]*

I married an archeologist because the older I grow, the more he appreciates me.

⟶ ⟵

Someone worked for me once who had a habit of telling people that they were "appreciated." For some reason or other this really got on my nerves. I used to think it was trite, contrived, perhaps even artificial, although I knew she was a good person and didn't have a mean bone in her body. She occasionally gave me cards with this expression, when I was busy in my world of practice and business and raising little babies on my own. I used to think what I really want is another body at the house, someone to make the dinner, someone to just give me a *break*. What good is a card when you're dying for an extra set of hands? If only I could turn the clock back now—I'd have those cards hanging all over the house just to get me through the day. Deep, deep down in my heart I feel I owe her an apology. I appreciate *her* now.

⟶ ⟵

PERCEIVE

*D*EFINITION:

to obtain knowledge of through the senses; to apprehend by the mind; to be convinced of by direct intuition; to discern; to understand; to remark; to note.

*E*TYMOLOGY:

Old French, *percevoir*; Latin *percipere*, from *per*, through, thoroughly + *capere*, to take, receive.

*Q*UOTATIONS

Not what we experience, but how we perceive what we experience, determines our fate.

—*Marie von Ebner-Eschenbach*[2]

To effectively communicate, we must realize that we are all different in the way we perceive the world, and use this understanding as a guide to our communication with others.

—*Tony Robbins*[2]

My kids always perceive the bathroom as a place where you wait it out until all the groceries are unloaded from the car.

—*Erma Bombeck*[1]

We are all born with the capacity to be perceptive, to receive information *thoroughly*. I don't know about you, but I certainly didn't pay much attention to its potential. I spent so *little* energy noticing the things, people, and events surrounding me. But this ability is like any other skill—it's like a muscle that can be strengthened and nourished, exercised and grown. But as I sit here writing this, I'm thinking about how incredibly *unperceptive* I remain most days. I still have to work hard at it, even at heeding those intuitive gut feelings that show up spontaneously. Discerning or sensing how my life can still be purposeful is simply hard for me to do every day, but I have no intention whatsoever of giving up on it.

CALM

*D*EFINITION:

(adjective) not stormy; still; serene; undisturbed by passion or emotion; not agitated or excited; tranquil; quiet in act or speech. (verb) to still or soothe.

*E*TYMOLOGY:

French, *calme*; Late Latin *cauma*, the heat of the sun; Greek καυμα *(kauma)*, great heat.

*Q*UOTATIONS

Many a calm river begins as a turbulent waterfall, yet none hurtles and foams all the way to the sea.

—*Mikhail Lermontov²*

Peace, it does not mean to be in a place where there is no trouble, noise, or hard work. It means to be in the midst of those things and still be calm in your heart.

—*Lady Gaga¹*

Nothing baffles the schemes of evil people so much as the calm composure of great souls.
—*Gabriel Riqueti Mirabeau*[3]

God promises a safe landing, not a calm passage.
—*Bulgarian proverb*[3]

In the world of medicine you learn to stay calm in very intense situations, like when you're resuscitating someone whose heart just stopped. Although I accomplished this task in my professional life, deep down inside I lived in a maelstrom of nonstop chatter, a state of constant self-criticism, of *what ifs, should haves, why didn't I's*—you name it. This continuous internal audio loop kept playing when my other outward functions shut down. When I was paralyzed by sadness and despair, I *never* felt calm. Now I've learned to work at it, to cultivate habits like meditation, exercise, paying attention to the serenity of nature. And I found out how important it is to unplug too. Don't think you'll master calmness when you sleep with your cell phone on the pillow beside you. It simply doesn't work that way.

DESTINY

$\mathscr{D}$EFINITION:

the fixed order of things; invincible necessity; fate; a resistless power or agency conceived of as determining the future, whether in general or of an individual.

$\mathscr{E}$TYMOLOGY:

Old French, *destiner*; Latin *destina*, a support, prop, from *de*, down + *stanare*, to cause to stand, set up.

$\sim\!\!\!\mathscr{W}\!\!\!\sim$

$\mathscr{Q}$UOTATIONS

We are not permitted to choose the frame of our destiny. But what we put into it is ours.

—*Dag Hammarskjold*[3]

There is a destiny that makes us brothers. No one goes his way alone; All that we send into the lives of others, Comes back into our own.

—*Edwin Markham*[3]

A person often meets his destiny on the road he took to avoid it.

—*Jean de la Fontaine*[2]

Let us resolve to be masters, not the victims, of our history, controlling our own destiny without giving way to blind suspicions and emotions.

—John Fitzgerald Kennedy[3]

So many famous people, so many quotations that I found, espouse a capacity to create our own destiny. This has always confused me. The definition makes the sense of predetermination in this word clear and brings to mind others like kismet and karma. So many things that happened to me were beyond my control, things that I certainly didn't plan for or design. I look *back* on all this as my destiny. So what, then, kept me standing? The key to unlocking yourself from the trapped and frozen feeling that occurs in an unexpected situation is in choosing how you *respond* to it. I learned that a considered, deliberate reaction—a choice to do your positive best when everything collapses around you—will make matters move toward a more fulfilling destiny.

DECIDE

*D*EFINITION:

to determine; to form a definite opinion; to come to a conclusion; to bring to a termination, as a question, controversy, struggle, by giving the victory to one side or party; to settle.

*E*TYMOLOGY:

Old French, *decider*; Latin *decidere*, from *de*, from, off + *caedere*, to cut.

*Q*UOTATIONS

The world will change for the better when people decide they are sick and tired of being sick and tired of the way the world is, and decide to change themselves.

—*Sidney Madwed*[3]

If you choose not to decide, you still have made a choice.

—*Neil Peart*[3]

The first step towards getting somewhere is to decide that you are not going to stay where you are.

—*John Pierpont Morgan*[3]

Before borrowing money from a friend decide which you need most.

—*Source unknown*[3]

⁓✕⁓

*D*uring my working years I made tens of thousands of decisions—mostly for others—based on my training, knowledge, and experience. It seems as if the more and more I did this, the less and less time I spent on things for *myself*. To make matters worse, many of the personal choices I made were not in my best interest. I was always in a hurry and often "settled" on something quickly because I felt pressured to do so, or because I just didn't take the time to think it through. I ended up paying a massive price for some actions that were taken in haste. I cut myself off from something, all right: better opportunities, healthier outcomes, safer or more predictable circumstances. Oh well, haven't we all! But decisions will be mine to make for a very long time to come, and I'm determined to do a much better job with them.

⁓✕⁓

EXPERIENCE

*D*EFINITION:

(noun) the effect upon the judgment or feelings produced by any event, whether witnessed or participated in; experimental or inductive knowledge; (verb) to make practical acquaintance with; to feel; to try personally; to be affected by.

*E*TYMOLOGY:

Old French *experience*; Latin *experientia*, a trial, and *experiri*, to try thoroughly, from *ex*, out + *periri*, to go through.

*Q*UOTATIONS

It has been my experience that folks who have no vices have very few virtues.

—*Abraham Lincoln*[2]

We are not human beings having a spiritual experience. We are spiritual beings having a human experience.

—*Pierre Teilhard de Chardin*[2]

Lying in bed would be an altogether perfect and supreme experience if only one had a colored pencil long enough to draw on the ceiling.

—*Gilbert K. Chesterton*[2]

⸎

The definition of this word gave me a whole new viewpoint. I simply didn't think of experience in terms of feelings or judgments; I associate it more with the concept of memories. My depression reduced me to a state of living in an emotional wasteland. At that point, a post-apocalyptic scene of gray rubble and ash took possession of my mind. It's said that we remember bad events more vividly than good ones, and for a longer period of time, as an adaptive means of protection against future threats. This image of the Hiroshima-like aftermath, this profound experience with a disease that risked my very life, now makes me think of the delicate lightness of ash and its value in fertilizing a tillable landscape. For me, it's been one of my better teachers.

⸎

MYSTICAL

*D*EFINITION:

remote from or beyond human comprehension; mysterious; baffling human understanding; unknowable.

*E*TYMOLOGY:

Old French *mystique*, via Latin from Greek μυστικοσ *(mustikos)*, from *mustes*, initiated person, and *muein*, close the eyes or lips; also, initiate.

M

*Q*UOTATIONS

It is the eternal truth in the political as well as the mystical body, that, where one member suffers, all the members suffer with it.

—*Junius*[3]

What I do deny is that you can build any enduring society without some such mystical ethos.

—*Herbert Read*[1]

So the supernatural becomes the mystical unknown—we refer to it as the unconscious, heaven, maybe even God.

—*William Shatner*[1]

⁓

I had a strict Catholic upbringing in the fifties and sixties, and actively rejected it when I escaped to the big city for college. Soon enough, science and rationality took over my life. I ignored and suppressed the little voice deep inside that kept reminding me that something else was "out there." I'm convinced now that my brushing aside the mystical aspects of life only contributed to my unbalanced state. Well, there came a point in time where I had to look the spiritual straight in the eye again. I made a conscious decision to study and embrace it, a decision that was instrumental in allowing me to move forward again. My faith in a higher power is still difficult for me to put in words, but there's no doubt in my mind that I wouldn't be here without it.

⁓

WELCOME

*D*EFINITION:

(noun) kind reception of a guest or newcomer; (verb) to salute with kindness; to receive and entertain hospitably and cheerfully; (adjective) producing gladness; grateful; free to have or enjoy gratuitously.

*E*TYMOLOGY:

Icelandic *velkominn*, welcome; Anglo-Saxon *wilcuma*, one who comes so as to please another.

*Q*UOTATIONS

If we had no winter, the spring would not be so pleasant; if we did not sometimes taste of adversity, prosperity would not be so welcome.
—*Anne Dudley Bradstreet*[3]

Welcome the task that makes you go beyond yourself.
—*Frank McGee*[3]

106 |

Defeat the fear of death and welcome the death of fear.
—*G. Gordon Liddy*[2]

If what happens does not make us richer, we must welcome it if it makes us wiser.
—*Samuel Johnson*[3]

Depression and pain eventually conditioned me to believe that I wasn't welcome anywhere—that people would rather not be around me. Not only did this complicate my life, but it also became somewhat of a self-fulfilling prophecy. For a span of several years, social isolation ruled my days. I'd certainly welcomed all kinds of people into my home and office and had enjoyed being hospitable in various and sundry circumstances. Since my life is different now, I try to actively welcome things that may be unanticipated or even difficult. I try to face them as best I can, while being kind to myself. And I've worked to be more secure in knowing that my true friends will provide welcome comfort in good times and bad, as I will always try to do for them.

PREPARE

to fit, adapt, or qualify for a particular purpose or condition;
to make ready; to provide; to put in order.

ETYMOLOGY:

Middle French *preparer*; from Latin *praeparare*, from *prae*,
beforehand + *parare*, to get ready.

QUOTATIONS

This is the precept by which I have lived: Prepare for the
worst; expect the best; and take what comes.
—*Robert E. Speer*[3]

A discovery is said to be an accident meeting a prepared
mind.
—*Albert Szent-Gyorgyi*[3]

By failing to prepare, you are preparing to fail.
—*Benjamin Franklin*[2]

There are two things in life for which we are never truly prepared: twins.

—Josh Billings[1]

✳

I believe that most of us are never totally prepared for the curveballs life throws at us. I had all kinds of safeguards in place for my children and me: a retirement plan, college funds, disability insurance—all assembled by me alone by the sweat of my own brow. Yet it all disappeared in a nightmare of bad advice, bad luck, and a fair degree of incompetence. I'm not young anymore, and once again find myself starting from scratch. I had to do what Robert Speer advised: I had to take what comes, take the ball and run with it. Not one of us can ever be fully prepared for unexpected and unforeseen loss or illness. But after we take a time out to assess the damage, it's time to get back in and finish the game.

✳

OPPORTUNITY

*D*EFINITION:

a time or place favorable for executing a purpose; a suitable combination of conditions; chance; fitness; convenience of situation.

*E*TYMOLOGY:

French *opportun*, timely; Latin *opportunus*, convenient, seasonable, from *ob*, near + *portus*, harbor, port.

*Q*UOTATIONS

I was seldom able to see an opportunity until it had ceased to be one.

—*Mark Twain*[3]

Wherever there is a human being, there is an opportunity for kindness.

—*Lucius Annaeus Seneca*[1]

It pays to know the enemy—not least because at some time you may have the opportunity to turn him into a friend.

—*Margaret Thatcher*[3]

Learn to listen. Opportunity could be knocking at your door very softly.

—*Frank Tyger*[3]

I was blessed with many wonderful opportunities in life—a chance to attend excellent schools, the miracle of having twins because of a marvelous fertility specialist, the freedom to practice my craft in a safe and beautiful place as I raised my family. But although the time, place, and circumstances surrounding my losses were not "favorable" or "suitable" by any means, I still saw them as another opportunity. I saw a chance, perhaps for the last time in my life, to learn a whole new set of skills including forgiveness, compassion for myself and for others, humility, austerity, and many more. I'm glad I listened to the little voice inside that told me to take that chance while I still could, and reminded me that I could still make something out of nothing while sailing forward once again toward future ports of call. I can only hope they'll be safer havens from now on.

TENACITY

*𝒟*EFINITION:

the quality or fact of being able to grip something firmly;
the quality or fact of being very determined; determination;
the quality or fact of continuing to exist; persistence.

*ℰ*TYMOLOGY:

Middle French *tenacite*; Latin *tenacitas*, from *tenax*, holding
fast.

*𝒬*UOTATIONS

The most difficult thing is the decision to act, the rest is
merely tenacity. The fears are paper tigers. You can do
anything you decide to do. You can act to change and
control your life; and the procedure, the process, is its own
reward.

—Amelia Earhart[2]

To succeed in life in today's world, you must have the will
and tenacity to finish the job.

—Chin-Ning Chu[2]

A wedding anniversary is the celebration of love, trust, partnership, tolerance and tenacity. The order varies for any given year.

—*Paul Sweeney*[2]

∽ℳ∽

There was a lawyer in Buffalo who bombarded cable TV with advertisements about his services. His claim to fame was that he was tenacious for his clients. Somehow this prompted me to visit this word. It took a lot of tenacity for me to emerge from a very dark place and begin to move forward. Tenacity and strength were what got me started. We each possess this quality to some degree; we need to call it up into our consciousness when needed, to remind ourselves that we determine our own fate. We have to be both persistent and consistent in our efforts to turn things around. I actually called that lawyer when everything went sour and I needed legal advice, but he had no interest in being tenacious for me! Luckily, that didn't sour me on the merits of this word.

∽ℳ∽

PRECIOUS

𝒟EFINITION:

of great value or worth; highly esteemed; dear; beloved; of great price.

𝓔TYMOLOGY:

French *precieux*; Latin *pretiosus*, valuable, from *pretium*, a price, value.

𝒬UOTATIONS

Nothing is more difficult, and therefore more precious, than to be able to decide.

—*Napoleon Bonaparte*[3]

It is possible to experience an awakening in this life through realizing just how precious each moment, each mental process, and each breath truly is.

—*Christy Turlington*[2]

Our emotional symptoms are precious sources of life and individuality.

—*Thomas More*[2]

The most precious things in speech are pauses.

—*Ralph Richardson*[2]

*P*ersonally, I think this word may suffer a bit from overuse, even sensationalism. We characterize anything at all as precious, from the banal to the sublime—jewels, keepsakes, memories, moments—even life itself! I think this dilutes its power. Where do we draw the line? I like to ask, "What would *you* choose if you could only label one thing in your life precious?" For that matter, what would I? I decided that I value my inner spirit enough to stay alive and to walk the path of healing and improvement. But deep inside I think that the most precious things I can conceive of are my children. I don't think it's my depression speaking when I say that I truly would lay down my life for them. That's just the price I would pay.

COURAGE

*D*EFINITION:

that quality of mind which enables one to encounter danger and difficulties with firmness, or without fear; valor; resolution; strength in the face of pain or grief.

*E*TYMOLOGY:

Old French *corage*; from Latin *cor*, the heart.

*Q*UOTATIONS

Man cannot discover new oceans unless he has the courage to lose sight of the shore.

—Andre Gide[3]

It isn't for the moment you are struck that you need courage, but for the long uphill climb back to sanity and faith and security.

—Anne Morrow Lindbergh[3]

More powerful than the will to win is the courage to begin.

—*Source unknown*[3]

Courage is the power to let go of the familiar.

—*Mary Bryant*[3]

They say it's virtually impossible to triumph over adversity without courage. When people hear about the pain and grief of my life and how I survived it, they often comment on how strong I am. I always admitted to this, but never regarded my actions as courageous. But where does it come from, since it can't just be *given* to you? I seem to have it in excess, but some have to look hard for it, dig for it deep inside, maybe clean it up a bit, brush up the roots, and feed and water it. When the first tiny sprout takes hold, you can take a ministep. The day after that, you try a full step, and before you know it, you're walking half a block. Then your courage takes you further and further until, before you even know it, you find yourself running into the wind.

TRANSCEND

DEFINITION:

to rise above; to exceed; to surpass; to be or go beyond the range or limits of (a field or activity or conceptual sphere).

ETYMOLOGY:

Latin *transcendere*, from *trans*, beyond + *scandere*, to climb.

QUOTATIONS

Desire is the starting point of all achievement, not a hope, not a wish, but a keen pulsating desire which transcends everything.

—*Napoleon Hill*[3]

No one can transcend their own individuality.

—*Arthur Schopenhauer*[3]

Like music and art, love of nature is a common language that can transcend political or social boundaries.

—*Jimmy Carter*[2]

ऀ

I never thought of this word in an active sense, but usually imagine an outside force—some sort of big hand in the sky—magically appearing to help someone transcend their circumstances. I never put much of an intentional spin on it. Studying and working in the world of hard science has given me a rather limited and almost-regimented kind of life that can impede transcendence. A comforting sense of security can be found behind the boundaries of logic and rationality, rules and regulations, of course, but this can also blind us to new possibilities, untried paths of healing, uncharted roads to a whole new world. We need to be kind to ourselves and remember that although the road is rocky and twisting, and the air is cold and damp, we can still find the power within us to climb that mountain ahead.

ऀ

PERFECT

*D*EFINITION:

(adjective) having all the properties or qualities requisite to its nature and kind; without flaw, fault, or blemish; right; highly suitable for someone or something; (verb) to finish or complete, so as to leave nothing wanting; make as good as possible.

*E*TYMOLOGY:

Old French *parfit*; Latin *perficere*, to complete, from *per*, thoroughly + *facere*, to make.

*Q*UOTATIONS

A gem cannot be polished without friction, nor a man perfected without trials.

—*Chinese proverb*[3]

Perfection is achieved, not when there is nothing more to add, but when there is nothing left to take away.

—*Antoine de Saint-Exupéry*[1]

It is only imperfection that complains of what is imperfect. The more perfect we are the more gentle and quiet we become towards the defects of others.

—*Joseph Addison*[2]

If the world was perfect, it wouldn't be.

—*Yogi Berra*[2]

This word has so many layers of hidden meaning that it makes me laugh out loud just thinking about it! It brings to mind all the time and energy I wasted pursuing the "perfect" life. Those keeping-up-with-the-Joneses things that I worked so hard to acquire turned out to be a true house of cards, a feather-light structure incapable of supporting the needs of my very soul. But this word's etymology allows me to see it in a different way. I now apply *perfect* to challenging situations and setbacks that come my way almost every day. They give me the chance to see things through as best as I can at the time. They provide opportunities to learn a new strength or to be grateful for the blessings I already have. The beauty of this word is that it now becomes distinctly achievable—we can all become perfect in everything we do by simply doing our very best in the circumstances that are given us.

BALANCE

*D*EFINITION:

(noun) equilibrium; steadiness; mental or emotional stability; a situation in which different elements are equal or in the correct proportions; (verb) put (something) in a steady position so that it does not fall; compare the value of (one thing) with another; establish equal or appropriate proportions of elements in.

*E*TYMOLOGY:

French *balance*; Latin *bilanx*, from *bi*, double + *lanx*, a platter, dish, scale of a balance.

*Q*UOTATIONS

The world is in balance. ... To light a candle is to cast a shadow.
—*Ursula K. LeGuin*[3]

A well-developed sense of humor is the pole that adds balance to your step as you walk the tightrope of life.
—*William Arthur Ward*[3]

One out of four people in this country is mentally imbalanced. Think of your three closest friends; if they seem OK, then you're the one.

—*Ann Landers*[1]

∾

*D*o you remember a moment in time when you encountered an idea or a concept that stopped you dead in your tracks, one that made you look at your life in a new and different way? I had such a moment when a shaman explained that there were four components of my human self: body, mind, spirit, and emotions. Up until that point I had only envisioned the first three. Somehow, separating out that emotional entity helped me focus on my depression and the work that was needed to heal. But all at once it struck me that it was the balance of the elements that was also needed, that this is what my job must be every day. It's something I had somehow lost track of. Equilibrium, steadiness, and stability—yup, it sure sounds good to me.

∾

RESOURCE

*D*EFINITION:

means of overcoming a difficulty; resort; a source of help or information; personal attributes and capabilities regarded as able to help or sustain one in adverse circumstances; available means or capabilities of any kind.

*E*TYMOLOGY:

French *ressource*, a new source, a spring, a recovery, from Latin *re*, again + *surgere*, to rise.

*Q*UOTATIONS

It is only when you despair of all ordinary means, it is only when you convince it that it must help you or perish, that the seed of life in you bestirs itself to provide a new resource.

—*Robert Collier*[3]

Never forget the three powerful resources you always have available to you: love, prayer, and forgiveness.

—*H. Jackson Brown Jr.*[1]

Life is constantly providing us with new funds, new resources, even when we are reduced to immobility. In life's ledger there is no such thing as frozen assets.

—*Henry Miller*[3]

If you're wondering what resources are available to you, you first have to take stock. Take an inventory—mental or otherwise—of what you have in reserve: money, people, ideas, beliefs, whatever! At my absolute lowest I believed I had nothing except my children, my car, and a boatload of memories. Then it occurred to me that my very life was in itself a resource, a repository of capabilities from which I could pick and choose the ones I needed to move forward. So make a list of what you've got for support, you never know when you'll need to consult it. But just don't forget to list yourself!

LISTEN

*D*EFINITION:

to give close attention with the purpose of hearing; to attend; to yield to advice; to give heed.

*E*TYMOLOGY:

Anglo-Saxon *hlystan*, to pay attention to, from Teutonic *hleus*, to hear.

*Q*UOTATIONS

Were we as eloquent as angels we still would please people much more by listening rather than talking.
—*Charles Caleb Cotton*[3]

The more faithfully you listen to the voices within you, the better you will hear what is sounding outside.
—*Dag Hammarskjöld*[3]

If you listen to your fears, you will die never knowing what a great person you might have been.
—*Robert H. Schuller*[2]

No man ever listened himself out of a job.

—Calvin Coolidge[3]

$\sim$

$\mathscr{I}$ made deliberate efforts to hone my listening skills when I took care of sick people, and it served me well. Ironically, when I tuned in to my own internal chatter it was all about the mistakes I was making, the things I didn't do well enough, my lack of sufficient willpower to take care of myself properly, etc. It didn't help that the electronic world ruled the spaces in between—I'm an NPR junkie, and then there's the TV, elevator music, CDs, you name it! It took me a long time to learn I had to listen to the *silence*. You can nurture this habit by meditating, by turning everything off for a while, by taking a walk in the woods, by daydreaming, or simply staring into space. In that silence I'm able to find the strength and resilience to move forward every day.

$\sim$

CONFIDENCE

*D*EFINITION:

trust; reliance; a feeling of self-sufficiency; such assurance as leads to a feeling of security; the state of feeling certain about the truth of something; the telling of private matters or secrets with mutual trust.

*E*TYMOLOGY:

Latin *confidere*, to trust fully, from *con*, with, fully + *fidere*, to trust.

*Q*UOTATIONS

If you have no confidence in self, you are twice defeated in the race of life. With confidence, you have won even before you have started.

—*Marcus Garvey*[3]

You have to have confidence in your ability, and then be tough enough to follow through.

—*Rosalynn Carter*[2]

Confidence is the feeling you have before you understand the situation.

—*Source unknown*[3]

I love the confidence that makeup gives me.

—*Tyra Banks*[2]

◇◇◇

*B*ecoming a doctor wasn't easy, but once I discovered I wasn't harming people too much I was able to develop confidence rather quickly. I felt comfortable with motherhood right away too, perhaps because of my own mother's example and because I waited a long time to become one myself. These outward appearances of self-assurance belied an internal doubt that allowed depression to take over my life. After over a half-century of living I had to actually *learn* confidence in my very worth as well as convince myself that I could rise from the ashes and heal. I chose to love and accept myself without blame or judgment, a method I'd used with others for years. I had to learn how to trust in myself above all.

◇◇◇

WATCH

*D*EFINITION:

(verb) to be awake; to be attentive or vigilant; to keep guard; to be expectant; to wait; to seek opportunity; to observe the actions or motions of, for any purpose; not to lose from sight and observation; to tend; to have in keeping.

*E*TYMOLOGY:

Anglo-Saxon *wacian*; from Anglo-Saxon *wacan*, to wake.

*Q*UOTATIONS

The few who do are the envy of the many who only watch.

—Jim Rohn[3]

A champion is someone who is bending over to exhaustion when no one else is watching.

—Anson Dorrance[1]

Don't watch the clock, do what it does. Keep going.

—Sam Levenson[3]

The best way to lose weight is to close your mouth—
something very difficult for a politician. Or watch your
food—just watch it, don't eat it.

—*Edward Koch*[1]

I love this word. It originated from the Anglo-Saxon
word for wake, and is also related to the word wait. It makes
sense to me. Aren't you often waiting while you're watching
out for something, and one would hope you're managing
to stay awake! Be that as it may, I know that *not* watching
carefully had gotten me in plenty of trouble over the years.
Many times I wasn't mindful enough, or wasn't always
on the lookout for a potential downside or risk. I was
frequently in a hurry, or felt a pressing sense of urgency
to make this or that decision. I suppose in my own way I
was actually asleep at the switch! Now watching is very
important to me, as I wait, sometimes quite impatiently,
for the right path to be revealed.

SUCCEED

$\mathscr{D}$EFINITION:

to obtain the object desired; to accomplish what is attempted or intended; to fall heir to; to come after; to follow.

$\mathscr{E}$TYMOLOGY:

French *succeder*; Latin *succedere*, to go beneath or under, from *suc*, under + *cedere*, to go.

$\mathscr{Q}$UOTATIONS

There is no comparison between that which is lost by not succeeding and that which is lost by not trying.

—Francis Bacon[3]

To make one good action succeed another is the perfection of goodness.

—Ali Ibn Abi Talib[2]

Don't settle for style. Succeed in substance.

—Wynton Marsalis[2]

If at first you don't succeed, find out if the loser gets anything.

—*William Lyon Phelps*[2]

My adult world appeared outwardly successful, but underneath no one was aware of the terrible sense of failure that colored my days. Those feelings of worthlessness, guilt, inadequacy—my constant traveling companions, the hallmarks of a depressed mind—seemed impossible to conquer. I then "succeeded" in losing everything I thought was important to me. What followed, though, was a new and much healthier outlook on life. I'm succeeding now because I *am* accomplishing what I'm attempting to do, which is to be grateful for what I have and to be forgiving, respectful, and loving to others. In striving to triumph in some very tough times, I'm finding the peace that follows.

GENUINE

𝒟EFINITION:

authentic; real; natural; true; not counterfeit, spurious, false, or adulterated.

ℰTYMOLOGY:

Latin *genuinus*, from *genu*, knee (with reference to the Roman custom of a father acknowledging paternity of a newborn child by placing it on his knee); later associated with *genus*, birth, race, stock.

$$\sim\!\!\mathcal{M}\!\!\sim$$

𝒬UOTATIONS

If we are genuine to ourselves then we will automatically be genuine to others, hence at our best.

—*Robert Spinelli*[1]

My guiding principles in life are to be honest, genuine, thoughtful and caring.

—*Prince William*[1]

Do not think that love, in order to be genuine, has to be extraordinary. What we need is to love without getting tired.

—*Mother Teresa*[1]

The spirit of self-help is the root of all genuine growth in the individual.

—*Samuel Smiles*[2]

✑

I was pretty well known for an unadulterated way of expressing myself—people always said I'd "tell it like it is." I looked upon this as being genuine, although I realize in retrospect that this undiplomatic approach could often be hurtful or offending. Things often seemed so obvious to me, I frequently wondered how others could see them differently. Studies show that people with depression can be uncannily accurate in their statements, judgments, or memories. They tend to neither exaggerate nor minimize things. This can be a valuable asset, of course, but at times my own position of certainty and assurance caused unnecessary pain. I've learned that I can be genuine to myself at a very deep level, but must set proper boundaries so that I don't hurt others in the process.

✑

AFFIRM

$\mathscr{D}$EFINITION:

to assert positively; to tell with confidence; to maintain as true; to offer (someone) emotional support or encouragement.

$\mathscr{E}$TYMOLOGY:

Old French *afermer*, to fix, secure; Latin *affirmare*, to make firm, from *ad*, to + *firmus*, strong.

$\mathscr{Q}$UOTATIONS

It is always easier to believe than to deny. Our minds are naturally affirmative.

—*John Burroughs*[3]

It's the repetition of affirmations that leads to belief. And once that belief becomes a deep conviction, things begin to happen.

—*Muhammad Ali*[1]

It is not necessary to deny another's reality in order to affirm your own.

—*Anne Wilson Schaef*

We've all heard about the benefits of using affirmations to change the way we think. They work because the unconscious mind, deep down inside, will follow what the conscious mind tells it. There was a period in my life when I wrote the phrase "I can do this" many, many times a day. I filled pages with it! On any given day, I might not have been sure what "this" actually was, but I was telling myself that I had the capacity to keep going, to move forward, to deal with that day's challenges and obstacles. When I felt my strength ebbing, I'd ask my son or a friend to affirm things with me, to remind me that I *was* getting better, that I could face the daily problems that at times seemed so insurmountable, that I would somehow see my way through. For me, the hardest part was picking up the pen to do the writing, but when I made myself, I began to feel the energy flow.

ACCEPT

𝒟EFINITION:

to receive with a consenting mind (something offered); to assent to; to approve; to acknowledge; to understand; to take upon oneself (a responsibility or liability).

𝓔TYMOLOGY:

Latin *acciptere*, to receive, from *ad*, to + *capere*, to take.

∽

𝒬UOTATIONS

Once we accept our limits, we go beyond them.
—*Brendan Francis Behan*[2]

We cannot change anything until we accept it. Condemnation does not liberate, it oppresses.
—*Carl Gustav Jung*[3]

We must accept finite disappointment, but never lose infinite hope.
—*Martin Luther King Jr.*[2]

The reason I talk to myself is because I'm the only one whose answers I accept.

—*George Carlin*[2]

✒

*W*hen things go wrong we can often take on a posture of resistance or denial. In my case, I found it virtually impossible to accept the fact that I had lost everything I'd built with my own hands. I spent all my energy trying to fight the unfairness, lies, and deceit that surrounded me, believing it was my duty to resist the nefarious powers that seemed to conspire against me. During my first group session in the psychiatric hospital a therapist reminded us in no uncertain terms that *life isn't fair.* Magically, once I accepted this, things got a lot easier. As I said yes to my situation, my expectations shifted. This simple act of acquiescence allowed me to move out from under the rock where I was hiding and to view my life in a new and different way.

✒

CONTACT

*D*EFINITION:

(noun) the state of physical touching; a meeting, communication, or relationship with someone; a person who may be approached for information or assistance; (verb) communicate with (someone), typically in order to give or receive information.

*E*TYMOLOGY:

Latin *contactus*, p.p. of *contingere*, to touch closely, from *con*, together + *tangere*, to touch.

*Q*UOTATIONS

Basic human contact—the meeting of the eyes, the exchanging of words—is to the psyche what oxygen is to the brain. If you're feeling abandoned by the world, interact with anyone you can.

—*Martha Beck*[2]

There is a healthful hardiness about real dignity that never dreads contact and communion with others however humble.

—*Washington Irving*[3]

140 |

A human being is only interesting if he's in contact with himself. I learned you have to trust yourself, be what you are, and do what you ought to do the way you should do it. You have to discover you, what you do, and trust it.

—*Barbra Streisand*[3]

Sometimes I think the surest sign that intelligent life exists elsewhere in the universe is that none of it has tried to contact us.

—*Bill Watterson*[1]

⁓⁓

"Let's stay in touch." "I'll touch base with you later." "Her story touched my heart." These common phrases are expressions of contact, of a communication through promises, plans, emotions, and ideas. When things got really rough for me, a support system based on contact somehow disappeared from my life. I became totally isolated and withdrawn. But what I missed most was the *physical* manifestation of this word. My twins left for college when everything fell apart and I was suddenly all alone, except for my little dog, Tippy. It was then that I was most grateful for her warm little body, her silky tail, and the wet kisses she bestowed on me in her rather begrudging fashion. We need to remember this basic human need for contact, which is a gift we can give with impunity to those who need it most.

⁓⁓

DIGNITY

*D*EFINITION:

the state of being worthy or honorable; elevation of mind or character; quality suited to inspire respect or reverence; stateliness.

*E*TYMOLOGY:

Old French *dignité*; Latin *dignitas*, worth, perhaps related to *decus*, esteem, and *decet*, it is fitting.

*Q*UOTATIONS

Dignity does not consist in possessing honors, but in deserving them.

—*Aristotle*[2]

Our dignity is not in what we do, but what we understand.

—*George Santayana*[3]

We rise in glory, as we sink in pride: where boasting ends, there dignity begins.

—*Edward Young*[3]

The worse indignity is to be given a bedpan by a stranger who calls you by your first name.

—*Maggie Kuhn*[3]

Human dignity *is* self-worth, self-esteem; it doesn't get any simpler than that. I was consumed by shame, humiliation, and guilt for several years. During that period, dignity seemed to go into hibernation mode. My rational mind continued to function, though, and kept on reminding me about the undignified state I was in! How awful is that? You have no idea how many times I begged to be stark, raving mad so that I wouldn't be so aware of my situation. My dignity made a slow but progressive return to the surface as I was helped along by the care of others and awoke once again to my own potential. Now that it's back, I've promised myself to keep better track of it.

PROTECT

*D*EFINITION:

to cover or shield from danger or injury; to defend; to guard; to preserve in safety.

*E*TYMOLOGY:

Latin *protegere*, from *pro*, before + *tegere*, to cover.

*Q*UOTATIONS

Boundaries are to protect life, not to limit pleasures.
—*Edwin Louis Cole*[3]

On this path effort never goes to waste, and there is no failure. Even a little effort toward spiritual awareness will protect you from the greatest fear.
—*Bhagavad Gita*[3]

Painting: The art of protecting flat surfaces from the weather and exposing them to the critic.

—*Ambrose Bierce*[1]

⌐*y*⌐

I freely take full credit for having done what mothers do best, which is to protect the health and safety of their children. My kids mean the world to me and are just the greatest gift I've ever received. But protecting them wasn't always easy, especially during a time when my son became the target of some intense bullying in middle school. All the money and success I'd achieved couldn't buy the minute-by-minute safety from verbal and physical taunts that I so craved for him. But the fortitude, forbearance, and determination that he displayed, despite his tender years, taught me a lot. When I was tormented by my own foes later on, I often thought of his persevering attitude and told myself that if he could do it, so could I. He doesn't take much credit for it, but I know that he helped to protect and preserve my very existence.

⌐*y*⌐

ENDURE

𝒟EFINITION:

to bear with patience; to suffer without opposition or without sinking under the pressure or affliction; to remain firm under; to last.

ℰTYMOLOGY:

Old French *endurer,* from Latin *in,* in + *durare,* to last.

𝒬UOTATIONS

What is to give light is to endure the burning.
—*Victor Frankl*[3]

Maturity is the capacity to endure uncertainty.
—*John Huston Finley*[3]

The final proof of greatness lies in being able to endure criticism without resentment.
—*Elbert Hubbard*[3]

One thing at a time, all things in succession. That which grows fast withers as rapidly; and that which grows slow endures.

—*J. G. Holland*[1]

⁓

How often do we ask ourselves, "How much suffering can one endure?" My joke answer used to be, "As much as one gets." I commonly associated the word endurance with physical pain, as opposed to the emotional or spiritual variety. I thought that, yes, people must *endure* the nasty sensations served up by their own bodies, and then congratulated myself on my own high pain tolerance. But I was born with that; it wasn't something I had to *work* at. At the height of my depression I consciously chose to live, to put effort into staying on this planet, to stick around longer, to *last*. I've got a different view of this word right now—it has a broader and wider application. When I think of the love and support that got me through the worst of times, I believe I can endure anything.

⁓

PRAISE

*D*EFINITION:

(verb) to commend; to display the excellence of; to glorify on account of perfections or excellent works; (noun) the joyful tribute of gratitude or homage rendered to the Divine Being; worship, particularly worship by song.

*E*TYMOLOGY:

Old French *preis*, price, merit; Latin *pretiare*, to price, prize, value.

*Q*UOTATIONS

Most of us, swimming against the tides of trouble the world knows nothing about, need only a bit of praise and encouragement—and we will make the goal.
—*Jerome P. Fleishman*[3]

It is no great thing to be humble when you are brought low; but to be humble when you are praised is a great and rare attainment.
—*St. Bernard*[3]

It is one thing to praise discipline, and another to submit to it.

—*Miguel de Cervantes*[2]

⸏

*H*aving spent twelve years in Catholic school as a child, I cannot separate this word from my memories of church and religious ritual. But it also reminds me of how I used praise as a powerful tool in raising my children. How much easier it was to get them to brush their teeth or eat the right foods when I cheered on their every move—until the teenage years, that is. At any rate, at least I'd laid the groundwork. Why is it that I don't remember being praised when I was a child? All I remember is the criticism, and I can't recall much in terms of overt commendation. I've been told this is typical of a depressive nature. But nothing can beat the compelling motivation of a well-delivered compliment, or anything else that expresses the merit and value of effort well spent. I believe praise is truly one of those things where a little bit goes a long way.

⸏

TEACH

*D*EFINITION:

to impart the knowledge of; to guide the studies of; to cause (someone) to learn or understand something by example or experience; encourage someone to accept (something) as a fact or principle.

*E*TYMOLOGY:

Anglo-Saxon *taecan*, show, present, point out; Anglo-Saxon *tacan*, a token; German *zeigen*, to show; Greek δειγμα *(deigma)*, sample.

*Q*UOTATIONS

Age should not have its face lifted, but it should rather teach the world to admire wrinkles as the etchings of experience and the firm line of character.

—*Ralph B. Perry*[3]

I'd rather learn from one bird how to sing than to teach ten thousand stars how not to dance.

—*E. E. Cummings*[3]

Those that know, do. Those that understand, teach.

—*Aristotle*[2]

＿*＿

I started my solo practice when I became a mother of twins, and these double duties kept my hands full for a long time. But as my children got older, I felt a need to give back to the next generation of practitioners and experienced an unrelenting urge to teach my craft. I had fond memories of the mentors who made an impact on me back in the day and thought about all the things they taught me that weren't found in textbooks. The opportunity to teach medical students was one of the reasons I left Pennsylvania, but when I finally got started I found that others did not necessarily share the intense curiosity I had about the diseases I treated. This upset me until I remembered all the classes I'd skipped, all the tests that I barely passed because I just didn't care about the subject matter. So in the process of teaching I became a student again. I learned patience and how to be less judgmental and more creative, more tolerant of the interests of others. I had to learn how to wait until I encountered that occasional student who got as excited about lymphocytes and mast cells as I was. I could then use my experience and knowledge in pointing out my hard-earned knowledge to a willing recipient.

＿*＿

COMFORT

*D*EFINITION:

(noun) a state of quiet enjoyment; freedom from pain, want, or anxiety; consolation in trouble; assistance. (verb) to impart strength and hope to; to encourage; to relieve; to console; to cheer.

*E*TYMOLOGY:

Old French *conforter*; Latin *confortare*, to fortify, from *con*, together + *fortis*, strong.

*Q*UOTATIONS

Comfort and prosperity have never enriched the world as much as adversity has.
—*Billy Graham*[2]

Cure sometimes, treat often, comfort always.
—*Hippocrates*[2]

A man cannot be comfortable without his own approval.
—*Mark Twain*[1]

When things are bad, we take comfort in the thought that they could always get worse. And when they are, we find hope in the thought that things are so bad they have to get better.

—*Malcolm Stevenson Forbes*[2]

ᴍ

A comfort zone is defined as "a behavioral state that is anxiety neutral," a set of circumstances that we create to make us feel secure. We like it there; we hesitate to operate outside of it because we fear the risk involved. Wouldn't it be nice if we could stay there forever? Of course, that's simply unfeasible. But these zones are like little prefab houses that we can quickly put together as the need arises. We can use tools such as patience, silence, meditation, exercise, or compassionate communication to build our shelter from the storm. Obviously, a strong gust of wind can tear it apart, but at that point we need to rebuild the zone, that refuge where we feel stable, knowing full well that things will change and the need to remake will arise again. And when we're back inside, all safe and sound and warm, we can reach out to comfort others as well.

ᴍ

PRODUCE

DEFINITION:

to bring forward; to bear; to generate; to cause to be or to happen; to manufacture; to originate, as an effect or result; make (something) using creative skills.

ETYMOLOGY:

Latin *producere*, to bring forward, from *pro*, forward + *ducere*, to lead.

QUOTATIONS

Dreams pass into the reality of action. From the action stems the dream again; and this interdependence produces the highest form of living.

—*Anaïs Nin*[1]

Gratitude is a quality similar to electricity; it must be produced and discharged and used up in order to exist at all.

—*Henry Ward Beecher*[1]

Adversity draws men together and produces beauty and harmony in life's relationships, just as the cold of winter produces ice-flowers on the windowpanes, which vanish with the warmth.

—Søren Kierkegaard[3]

No matter how hard you referee, parenting will eventually produce bizarre behavior, and I'm not talking about the kids. Their behavior is always normal.

—Bill Cosby[2]

_I_ believe that a fundamental role of human beings is to produce, to make something—anything from a paper clip to a new theory on the cosmos. After decades of high output I spent years in a state of massive stagnation because of my depression. Imagine my shock when I saw myself in an almost-total state of nonproductiveness! At that point I had to watch and wait, believing that something would appear and "lead" me out of the darkness and into a better place. The going was tough, there was no magic bullet, and I had to collect and assemble the little bits and pieces to put the puzzle of my life back together again. I had to have faith and trust that help would arrive. If you're feeling ineffective, just make a list of the little things you make happen each day, even something as simple as holding open a door for someone. You might be surprised at how much you produce.

ADJUST

$\mathcal{D}$EFINITION:

to fit; to bring into proper relations; to put in order; to settle or bring to a satisfactory state, so that parties are agreed in the result; to adapt or become used to a new situation.

$\mathcal{E}$TYMOLOGY:

Old French *ajoster*; Latin *adiuxtere*, to put side by side, from *ad*, to, by + *iuxtare*, near to.

$\mathcal{Q}$UOTATIONS

The pessimist complains about the wind; the optimist expects it to change; the realist adjusts the sails.
—*William Arthur Ward*[2]

There are things I can't force. I must adjust. There are times when the greatest change needed is a change of my viewpoint.
—*Denis Diderot*[2]

The best measure of a man's honesty isn't his income tax return. It's the zero adjust on his bathroom scale.
—*Arthur C. Clarke*[2]

Is there anything in our world that doesn't need adjustment, that doesn't need to be "settled in a satisfactory state"? It's a vital part of existence for everything from atoms to galaxies. You might want to ask yourself how you adapt to the inevitable changes that occur in life. Do you anticipate them, perceive them, and move with them, or do you wait for outside forces and events to put you where you may not want to be? I used to criticize myself for not taking as active a role as I could have in adjusting to devastating circumstances, but I've learned to be kinder to myself now. Some of these things were just too large to take on alone. I've since made a conscious decision to stay more in sync with my inner GPS, to stay as near to its signals as I can, so that I'm ready when adjustment becomes necessary. Those massive changes that took place in my life, and that I was able to process successfully, served a useful purpose: to reinforce and augment the adaptive skills that each of us carries within us.

EXPLORE

*D*EFINITION:

to seek for or after; to strive to attain by search; to look wisely and carefully for; to examine or evaluate (an option or possibility); to inquire into or discuss (a subject) in detail.

*E*TYMOLOGY:

Latin *explorare*, to search out, lit. to make to flow out, from *ex*, out + *plorare*, to make to flow, weep.

*Q*UOTATIONS

Explore your mind, discover yourself, then give the best that is in you to your age and to your world. There are heroic possibilities waiting to be discovered in every person.

—*Wilferd A. Peterson*[2]

Fear is a question. What are you afraid of, and why? Just as the seed of health is in illness, because illness contains information, your fears are a treasure house of self-knowledge if you explore them.

—*Marilyn Ferguson*[2]

It's important for the explorer to be willing to be led astray.

—Roger van Oech[3]

~%~

*L*earning new things is one of my passions, and I think we learn best when we do it with a sense of exploration. I loved delving into details about immunology, molecular biology, and the myriad miraculous workings of the human body. But I also became familiar with leather saddles when my daughter took up equestrian sports, and discovered the world of colors and fabrics, flats and renderings, when my son became a fashion designer. For years while doing this, though, I neglected to explore my inner self, to "look wisely and carefully" for the strengths and resources I could nurture and turn to when the going got rough. I came to self-inquiry a little late in life, but once I did, I found that the answers and assistance I was searching for all along began to flow in earnest.

~%~

POSITIVE

*D*EFINITION:

existing in fact; expressing or implying affirmation, agreement, or permission; constructive, optimistic, or confident; with no possibility of doubt; showing progress or improvement.

*E*TYMOLOGY:

French *positif*; Latin *positus*, p.p. of *ponere*, to place.

*Q*UOTATIONS

Our lives are not determined by what happens to us but by how we react to what happens, not by what life brings to us, but by the attitude we bring to life. A positive attitude causes a chain reaction of positive thoughts, events, and outcomes. It is a catalyst; a spark that creates extraordinary results.

—*Source unknown*[3]

An individual's self-concept is the core of his personality. It affects every aspect of human behavior; the ability to learn, the capacity to grow and change. ... A strong, positive self-image is the best possible preparation for success in life.

—*Joyce Brothers*[3]

Nothing really matters except what you do now in this instant of time. From this moment onwards you can be an entirely different person, filled with love and understanding, ready with an outstretched hand, uplifted and positive in every thought and deed.

—*Eileen Caddy*[3]

It was the advice of a holistic therapist that gave me the impetus to investigate the positive. It was the simple exercise of extracting positive words from a book and writing them down that began a process of healing and recovery from depression, a path that I am still pursuing today. The work is difficult. For me, it's been harder than all the courses, examinations, and certifications I took to become a medical doctor. It's been harder than being a single parent of twins. I've chosen to "place" myself here, right now, and to try and make the best of this moment without undue concentration on the future or the past. But the rewards of self-knowledge, self-love, acceptance, and forgiveness have made it all worthwhile. There's simply nothing else left to say.

ACKNOWLEDGMENTS

I am grateful for the financial assistance provided by the Middletown Commission for the Arts, which awarded me a grant to help publish this book. This happened right after I moved into town and was a big factor in boosting my confidence and perseverance when I needed it most.

I would also like to thank my therapists at the Carrier Clinic in Belle Meade, New Jersey, who took my hand when I was in a dark place of despair and helped me to take those first few baby steps.

After beginning the book I sent the first few words out to friends and acquaintances for comments. Their *positive* feedback spurred me to keep going, when my mind was still very muddled and I didn't think I could make it. Thanks to all of you: Joy Crawford, Josh Dayton, Kristy Gasiweicz, Betsy Hare, Lisa Herrmann, Jim Miller, and others. I owe so much to Ann Sweet for her ongoing support, and for giving me a home when I lost mine.

I appreciate my new friends in Connecticut who accepted me when I came out to them with my story, and who also encouraged me to finish the process: Brigitte Botnick, Cassandra Day, Ann Gawlack, Helena Grey, Nancy Meinke, Andrea Vassallo, Patrick Connelly, and the lifeguards at the Northern Middlesex YMCA.

Thanks to old friends who came out of the woodwork to support me: Linda Alexander, Paula Rothaus, Joe Engel, Garry Ritter, Fran Sica, Sharon Gligora, and Cindy Morningstar. Linda, you know what a difference your generosity and yoga sessions made! And blessings to my good friend Jenny Bell, who provided so much help in many ways from way down there in South Carolina, and to Paul and Ahni Atkins for that transformative week on the mountain.

Thanks to my friends at the Russell Library: Brandie Doyle, Jason Neely, Jim Kubat, and Bob Carlson. Cathy Ahern, thank you for the wonderful services you and your colleagues provide, and for showing me a way out of my etymology mess!

Much gratitude is due to my gifted therapist, Alissa Wurtzel. And my vision could not have been completed without the support of Kimberly Barcello, my true soul sister, whose artistic input and ideas were so insightful and perfect. My acupuncturist, Dr. Stephen Greenberg, grounded me as I slogged through the rewrite and revisions. Dr. Kimberly DeWire and her staff helped me smile again.

But I am most grateful for my twins, Corby and Morgaine Enfiejian, who never abandoned me, who stepped up to the plate when their lives were turned upside down, and who withstood the storm of loss and turmoil to become the most wonderful and beautiful people that a mother could ever have. I can never love or thank you enough!

APPENDIX –
WORDS BY ALPHABET

REFERENCES

The word definitions are from the following source:
http://www.gutenberg.org/files/29765/29765-8.txt

The word etymologies are from the following source:
Skeat, Walter W. 1909. *An Etymological Dictionary of the English Language.* Oxford: Clarendon Press.

The quotation references can be found at the following websites:
1. http://www.quotesandpoem.com/
2. http://www.brainyquote.com/
3. http://www.quoteland.com/
4. http://www.lyrics007.com/John%20Lennon%20Lyrics/Imagine%20Lyrics.html

NOTES

NOTES

NOTES

NOTES